Physical Characteristics of the Cardigan Welsh Corgi

(from the The Kennel Club breed standard)

Body: Chest moderately broad with prominent breast bone. Body fairly long and strong, with deep brisket, well sprung ribs. Clearly defined waist. Topline level.

Tail: Like a fox's brush, set in line with the body and moderately long (to touch or nearly touch ground).

Coat: Short or medium of hard texture. Weather-proof, with good undercoat. Preferably straight.

Hindquarters: Strong, well angulated and aligned with muscular thighs and second thighs, strong bone carried down to feet, legs short when standing, hocks vertical when viewed from side and rear.

Size: Height: ideal 30 cms (12 ins) at shoulder. Weight in proportion to size with overall balance the prime consideration.

Feet: Round, tight, rather large and well padded. All dewclaws to be removed.

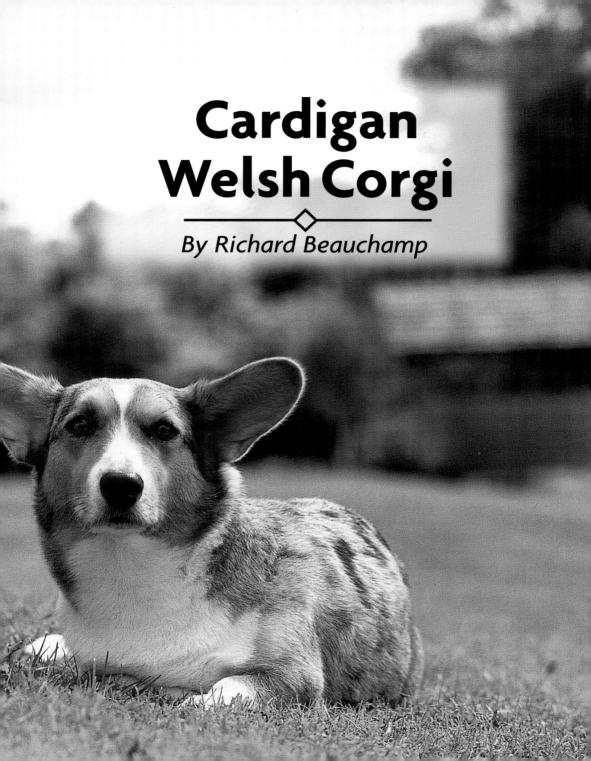

Cardigan Welsh Corgi

By Richard Beauchamp

CONTENTS

PUBLISHED IN THE UNITED KINGDOM BY:

INTERPET
PUBLISHING
Vincent Lane, Dorking, Surrey RH4 3YX England

ISBN 1-903098-98-X

PHOTOGRAPHS BY ISABELLE FRANÇAIS
with additional photos by Norvia Behling, TJ Calhoun, Carolina Biological Supply,
Lisa Croft-Elliott, Doskocil, James Hayden-Yoav, James R Hayden, RBP, Carol Ann Johnson,
Bill Jonas, Dwight R Kuhn, Dr Dennis Kunkel, Mikki Pet Products, Phototake,
Jean Claude Revy, Dr Andrew Spielman, Karen Taylor and Alice van Kempen.
Original illustrations by Patricia Peters.

The publisher wishes to thank Carla Hughs, Lisa Croft-Elliott,
Kathleen and Richard Hall, Robin M Frady, Gayle Garvin, Lynn Stoltzman, M Simermeyer,
M Magnus, as well as those not listed and the rest of the owners for allowing their
dogs to be photographed for this book.

The lesser known, but equally charming and loveable Corgi, the Cardigan Welsh Corgi possesses many different characteristics from the more popular Pembroke Welsh Corgi.

History of the
CARDIGAN WELSH CORGI

In Great Britain the name 'Corgi' will immediately evoke mental pictures of the short-legged and short-tailed little fellows that are so often seen behind, around and in front of members of the Royal family out on an afternoon's stroll. There are a few dog fanciers that respond to the word by asking, 'Which Corgi, the short-tailed or long?'

Two quite different dogs carry the name Corgi in their official designation—the Pembroke Welsh Corgi and the lesser known Cardigan Welsh Corgi. What very few people understand, however, is that the two are not simply different varieties of the same breed nor is tail length (or absence) the only distinguishing characteristic that separates the two.

The Cardigan and Pembroke trace their lineage back to entirely different ancestors, and these predecessors dictate much of what constitutes the differences in appearance and temperament that exist in the two breeds to this day. Although the Pembroke Corgi is by far the more popular of the two breeds, popularity is one of the last considerations that should be

> ### DID YOU KNOW?
> The herding instinct, so much a part of the Cardigan Corgi character, can be traced back through thousands of generations to the breed's wolf origins. Wolves cleverly 'rounded up' the animal they were after and separated it from the herd. When this was accomplished, they brought the animal to the ground and devoured it. It was through man's breeding genius that a dog was developed that was equipped with all of the herding abilities and instincts of its wolf ancestors but that was not compelled to kill and devour the livestock it herded.

taken into account when a breed is selected to become a member of one's family.

One of the major goals of this book is to enlighten the reader in regard to breed suitability when it comes time to select a household companion. Another is to bring the Cardigan Welsh Corgi out from behind the shadow of its more popular cousin, the Pembroke, to give the reader an opportunity to see the many sterling characteristics of this gentle and devoted result of British stockmanship.

In order to fully understand the essence of the Cardigan and how it differs from its cousin, one must really have a working knowledge of both breeds as well as why these differences exist. The following pages will attempt to reveal just that. In order to do so, however, we must go back in time—back to when man first began his relationship with the wild creature of the forest that was to become known as his 'best friend.' That relationship has grown to become one that man shares with no other living thing beyond his own species.

That first meeting was between Mesolithic man and the wolf. It began over 10,000 years ago. As early man matured into the intelligent and civilised being he is today, the wolf accompanied him through his transitions to become both servant and guardian. *Canis lupus*, the wolf, would become *Canis familiaris*, the dog.

CANIS LUPUS TO CANIS FAMILIARIS

Controversy exists as to whether today's domestic dog descended solely from the wolf family or if an admixture of jackal and other wild canine blood assisted in this transition. There is no doubt, however, that the four different branches of the wolf family stand as the cornerstone for all dogs included under the term *Canis familiaris* or *Canis domesticus*.

These four groups have been given different names by different historians, but Richard and Alice Fiennes' *The Natural History of*

Dogs categorises descendants of ancient dog as the Mastiff Group, the Dingo Group, the Greyhound Group and the Northern Group. The Mastiff and Northern Groups are the ones that figure most significantly in Corgi history, but it is of benefit to be aware of the characteristics of the other two groups as well in that neither of the Corgis can claim to be entirely pure in their descendency.

The Mastiff Group descended primarily from mountain wolves of the Tibetan wolf type and includes many of the dogs in today's Gundog Group classification, such as the spaniels and setters. The true scent-hunting hounds and mastiff-type dogs also descend from this group. There is evidence that some of the breeds in this group carry the blood of the spitz or Northern Group of wolves as well.

Typical of the Mastiff Group is a tendency to produce large floppy ears, a heavy muzzle and an obvious stop. A dog's stop is the depression or step down in the topline of the head, situated almost centrally between the eyes where the skull meets the upper jaw. These characteristics and several others will have increased significance as we trace the development of the Cardigan Welsh Corgi down from its *Deutsche Bracken* (German scenthound) ancestry.

The Dingo Group descended from the Asian wolf and includes the Basenji, the Rhodesian Ridgeback (albeit with many crosses to European breeds) and many of the pariah breeds existing in the Near, Middle and Far East as well as in Africa. Even in their least domesticated stage, this group appears to have been far more tractable and easily able to coexist with mankind.

The Greyhound Group claims an extremely fleet-of-foot Asian wolf relative as its source. Here we find all the sighthounds, with the Afghan Hound, the Borzoi, the Irish Wolfhound and the Greyhound among them.

Finally, we have the Northern Group, claiming the Northern Wolf as its predecessor. Included here

GENUS *CANIS*

Dogs and wolves are members of the genus *Canis*. Wolves are known scientifically as *Canis lupus* while dogs are often known as *Canis domesticus*. Dogs and wolves are known to interbreed. The term *canine* derives from the Latin derived word *Canis*. The term *dog* has no scientific basis but has been used for thousands of years. The origin of the word 'dog' has never been authoritatively ascertained.

DID YOU KNOW?

The Cardigan Welsh Corgi was bred to work both mean-spirited cattle and easily frightened sheep in the harshest of environments. This required a dog of great versatility—rugged enough in physique and temperament to stand up to the cattle but tractable and gentle enough to handle the far more timid sheep. This unique temperament is a hallmark of the breed to this day.

are most of the breeds associated with the extreme conditions of the cold climates. Among them we find the Arctic types, the terriers and the spitz breeds. The Pembroke Corgi is included in this group through its spitz ancestors.

Early man had little need to train the *wolf-cum-dog* descendants of this group to herd the livestock he kept. Wolves had been rounding up and separating their prey for countless centuries. Man's task was to produce a herder that would not bring down and devour what it herded! It appears descendants of the more docile Dingo Group had influence in this respect.

'HORSES FOR COURSES'

The frigid and often entirely inhospitable conditions of the Scandinavian countries dictated that the earliest inhabitants conserved in all things, including the dogs they kept. The Scandinavian breeds were hardy working breeds—some were markedly hound types of varying sizes, while others were made up of spitz descendency.

There is documented evidence that the Vikings took along their dogs on their journeys across the North Sea to Wales. One need only look at some of the breeds native to the Scandinavian countries to see how they might have influenced the development of the two Corgis in the British Isles. No one who has even a smattering of knowledge in regard to the development of the many breeds of dog that exist today could possibly deny the profound influence Great Britain has had in the world of pure-bred dogs.

'Horses for courses' is an old concept used by British stockmen in the development of many kinds of prized livestock. Translated into layman's terms, this simply means choosing a formula that will produce a horse best suited to the terrain of the region in which the animal will work. This breeding formula applied not only to horses but also to all stock, and was the basis upon which many of Great Britain's outstanding dog breeds were developed.

Pembrokeshire and Cardiganshire were agricultural areas in Wales. The farms were primarily set among the rather infertile and rocky hills. In addition, the weather was nothing short of inhospitable—often wild, wet and windy. A breed of tough black cattle was developed to cope with these difficult conditions.

Fences to confine these surly beasts were not practical or affordable. Regardless, the cattle had to be located and brought in so that they could be milked. This was a feat beyond the capability of the owners of the herds. They found a herding dog not only practical but, in so many cases, absolutely essential. There was little food available to maintain a large dog; plus, a large dog was not practical around the ill-tempered cattle. Flying hooves could easily land a well-directed rear kick to the head of a large dog.

What was needed was a small dog, short enough to duck under those flying hooves. The ingenious breeding talent of the Welsh farmers accomplished just that. The low stature of these dogs allowed them to nip at a reluctant beast's leg just above the hoof, while moving forward at the same time and in the same direction as the hoof. The agile little dogs simultaneously swerved slightly to the right or left, depending upon which hoof was grasped.

The natural inclination on the part of cattle was to strike rearward at the spot at which they were attacked. However, the

The Pembroke Welsh Corgi descends from spitz dogs and does not have a tail, giving the rear quarters its characteristic stumpy appearance.

BRAIN AND BRAWN

Since dogs have been inbred for centuries, their physical and mental characteristics are constantly being changed to suit man's desires for hunting, retrieving, scenting, guarding and warming their masters' laps. During the past 150 years, dogs have been judged according to physical characteristics as well as functional abilities. Few breeds can boast a genuine balance between physique, working ability and temperament.

clever dog was already out of the way. This is not to say that the dog never miscalculated, but, even if he did, the flying hoof would still lash out above the low-stationed herder's head.

The dogs' flat skulls were not a coincidence; rather, they were selected for by the farmers to assist in this technique of evasion. These dogs had to be tough little dogs because the nature of the beasts with which they worked and the weather in which they worked demanded it. A short, protective, weather-resistant coat was a must, for the conditions were all too often wet and muddy.

The inhabitants of Pembrokeshire and Cardiganshire went about their separate ways throughout the years to develop the kind of dog that was best suited to performing the required

tasks under the conditions that existed in their respective areas. The Welsh called these dogs 'Corgi.' The name Corgi generally meant 'cur dog' or, alternately, 'dwarf dog' in Welsh. Neither name was used in the derogatory sense, but rather to describe a small working type of dog.

It is believed that Cardiganshire folk used native British stock that may have been influenced by either Scandinavian or Central European hounds. The people in Pembrokeshire worked with dogs whose ancestors were thought to be primarily Scandinavian spitz breeds.

CARDIGANSHIRE'S CORGI

In Cardiganshire, the Corgi was also known as *Ci Llathaid*, which meant 'by the yard' and related to the Welsh measurement of a yard, which is 40 inches (101.5 cms) long. The dogs were larger than those of their neighbours in nearby Pembrokeshire. They also were considerably longer in body, their front legs were bowed and they had long bushy tails. They also stood on large round feet. They were often blue merle or brindle in colour and, in most cases, had large drooping ears.

At least one theory of the Cardigan Corgi's history cites the scenthound breeds as having had great influence. Scenthounds are thought to have been brought from Central European countries to Wales as early as 1200 BC. If these hounds arrived at that early date, they were undoubtedly of the German *Deutsche Bracken* type. If they arrived at a later date, the ancestors could well have been the German Dachshund or Teckel, which had been developed from the *Deutsche Bracken* dogs.

The hounds were said to have been crossed with the existing 'heeling' breeds of Wales. The resulting descendants were said to have had long bodies, bowed legs and large feet that turned out, as well as the typical scenthound's pendant ear.

Somewhere in the late 1800s, the Cardiganshire farmers began to replace their cattle with much more economically maintained herds of sheep. The cattle-heeling instincts of their Corgi proved too harsh for the easily frightened sheep, so they resorted to crosses with the less aggressive old Welsh Collie. It is believed that this is where the blue merle colour was introduced into the Cardigan gene pool.

There are many theories for the metamorphosis of the early hound-like Cardigan Corgi into a breed similar in some respects to its cousin, the Pembroke Corgi. Some believe it was done entirely without Pembroke crosses but rather through frequent breedings back to the indigenous Welsh herding breeds, which were prick-eared and more spitz-like in

The Swedish Vallhund is a cattle herder from the Vastergotland plains in Sweden. The forest dog resembles the Corgi except in colour. Owner, Lisa Croft-Elliott.

DID YOU KNOW?

Cardigan and Pembroke Corgis originally competed against each other for Challenge Certificates and, early on, it was the Pembrokes who walked off with the lion's share of the wins. However, at the Pwllheli show in 1929, a male Cardigan named Golden Arrow and a female Cardigan named Nell of Twyn turned the tables and brought home the CCs.

appearance. Others believe that the Pembroke dog had influence on the changes that came about for the dog from Cardiganshire. Only time and further archaeological discoveries will ever solve the mystery.

The hound blood in its background gave the Cardiganshire dog a marked determination of character so that they were seldom distracted from their assigned duties. This same hound blood gave the dogs a degree of serenity and gentleness around humans that endeared them to all members of the family, young and old.

At any rate, the dogs from Cardiganshire worked hard in the fields all day and protected their families from danger at night by

sounding the alarm. It was not unusual for the dogs to serve as 'nannies' for the children when the parents were away working in the fields. Had they been able, old fanciers of the breed say, they would have been put to scrubbing the laundry and cooking the meals.

These farming families could never have imagined that their beloved 'cur dogs' would one day be petted and pampered show dogs with nothing more to do than entertain their owners. The lowly Corgi from Cardiganshire was destined indeed for a life of comfort and convenience, the likes of which their farm-bound owners would never have been able to conceive.

THE PEMBROKESHIRE CORGI

In order to more fully understand the distinguishing differences that exist in the temperament and physique of the two Corgis, one must understand why they exist. Thus, a brief look at the development of the Corgi from Pembrokeshire is necessary. There seems to be

The Pembroke Welsh Corgi possesses a typical alertness and more compact size.

little doubt that the *Vastgotaspets* (Swedish Vallhund), developed from native spitz breeds in Sweden, had an important role in the development of the Pembroke Welsh Corgi. Whether it was the breeds native to Wales that may have influenced the development of the Vallhund, or the Swedish breeds serving as the cornerstone for the Corgi, will, at least for the present, remain another Corgi mystery to be solved. However, few doubt the connection between the Corgi and the Vallhund.

The Pembrokeshire Corgi was alternatively called *Ci Sodli*, which meant 'to heel,' or work livestock from behind by nipping at the heels. The dog was smaller than its cousin from Cardiganshire, was much more compact and had front legs that were fairly straight by comparison. Usually the Pembrokeshire dog was born without a tail. If one was born with a tail, it was docked. The head did not much differ from the Cardiganshire dog, but often the coat of *Ci Sodli* was shorter and smoother, and the ears were smaller.

The spitz blood coursing through the veins of the Pembrokeshire dogs gave them a decided edge and alertness. Nothing was apt to escape their notice nor would any intruder be allowed to pass unannounced.

THE CORGIS BECOME SHOW DOGS

Until the early 1920s, both Corgis led hard-working but contented lives on the farms. However, in about 1925, their destiny took an

DID YOU KNOW?

Dogs of the unique and attractive blue merle colour in the Cardigan Corgi had completely disappeared by the end of World War II. It is only through the hard work of breed doyen Thelma Gray that the gene for this colour was tracked down, and through controlled and persistent experimental breeding that the colour was revived.

abrupt turn. Several Corgi owners gathered at a local pub and decided that their dedicated companions should be included in dog shows.

Capt. J H Howell called a meeting of breed fanciers and the Welsh Corgi Club was organised. Pedigrees were written down from memory and breed standards were agreed upon. Ten dogs were given 'official' recognition as members of the breed.

The two Corgis, which up to that point had not yet been bred 'for looks,' began to appear at the local shows. The dogs ran the gamut of sizes and shapes, but a club was founded with a healthy 59-member charter group. These founding fanciers were interested only in the dog from Pembrokeshire, and it was that breed and that look that was promoted.

For the next decade, both types—Pembrokeshire and Cardiganshire (later shortened to Pembroke and Cardigan)—were considered as two varieties of the same breed, and interbreeding took place. Both were shown in the same classes at dog shows and registered as the same breed.

Early exhibitors recall terrible rows between the Cardigan and Pembroke people. Shows were judged by specialists and when Pembroke breeders judged, only Pembrokes won. Cardigan people were no less loyal to their breed

when they were called upon to judge.

Championship status was first granted Welsh Corgis in 1928 at the Cardiff show, but the two were still shown as one breed. The first champion in the breed, either Pembroke or Cardigan, was the red-and-white Pembroke female, Shan Fach, who annexed the title in 1929.

Each group felt theirs was the true Corgi type and the question was never settled nor was peace restored until 1934 when The Kennel Club in Great Britain granted separate breed status. At the time of separation, 59 Cardigans were registered versus 240 Pembrokes. Dividing the breed led to the difficult task of deciding to which of the two breeds each dog belonged. Often it was decided simply by the owner's choosing with which breed he or she wanted to be associated.

Five pairs of Challenge Certificates (CCs) were provided the Cardigan Corgis in 1935. A dog named Glantowy won his championship at The Kennel Club show held at the Crystal Palace in 1936, where the two breeds were shown separately.

The Cardigan was especially vulnerable to the two World Wars. Registrations dropped to only 11 for the year 1940 and even at the end of the Second World War, in 1945, registrations stood at 61, only 2 more than at the time of

Today the two Welsh Corgi breeds are decidedly different, and both Cardigans and Pembrokes are known to win in major group competition.

initial acceptance in 1934.

Still, owing to the indomitable spirit of the British fancy, both breeds did manage to survive the wars. Without missing a beat, the Welsh Corgi League, which had been founded by Thelma Gray in 1938, organised a gala Championship Show. The show was held at Buckingham Gate in London, where the Pembrokes were joined by the Cardigan Welsh Corgi Association.

Throughout the years, the Cardigan Corgi has not kept pace with the popularity afforded the Pembroke. Many of those favouring the long-tailed fellow appreciate that fact and consider the slow pace a distinct advantage, not wanting to see their breed become a 'fad' and fall into the wrong hands.

Other fanciers feel the breed deserves more recognition both as show dogs and as household companions. One of these is the late Mrs Thelma Gray, whose Rozval prefix is held in high regard by fanciers of both breeds. Mrs Gray is quoted as having said, 'I have always thought that it was a very great pity that the two breeds were named as they have been. Had the Cardigan Welsh Corgi become known as Welsh Dogs or Welsh Heelers I believe that their unique and endearing characteristics would have carried them to fame in the world of dogs long since.'

Characteristics of the
CARDIGAN WELSH CORGI

People are attracted to the Cardigan Corgi for many reasons. The Cardigan has a big-dog personality in a moderately sized package—a package that is ideal for most average homes. Other owners rave about the Cardigan's intelligence and his ability to understand and respond to those he loves. The breed seems to have a built-in mechanism that makes it an especially devoted companion and protector of children. The Cardigan has all of these wonderful personality traits, plus a wide range of beautiful colours and markings from which to choose.

All of these characteristics are valid in assessing the merits of the breed. However, they alone do not constitute reason enough for anyone to rush out to buy a Cardi. The prospective owner must do a little self-evaluation as well.

This is not a breed that can be put outdoors in a pen and attended to only when the owner has the time or notion to do so. A Cardigan can be a great companion and close friend for its entire lifespan, but only if the owner is ready to invest the time

and patience required to bring the dog to its full potential.

Just about all puppies are cuddly and cute; Cardi pups especially so. Their little 'one-ear-up-and-one-ear-down' waggy-tail personalities make them well nigh irresistible. Puppies are the subject of calendars and greeting cards printed around the world each year. It is important to realise, however, that a Cardigan Corgi puppy will spend only a very small part of its day sitting around looking cute. The far greater part of the day will be spent investigating, digging, chewing, eating, relieving itself and needing to go outdoors and

DID YOU KNOW?
Cardis are not inherently quarrelsome but they will not tolerate aggression on the part of other dogs. A Cardigan will not back down to a bully, no matter how large and imposing that bully might be. A leash and a collar are absolute musts any time your Corgi is not in your home or within the confines of your fenced-in property.

DIFFERENCES IN CORGIS

There are many differences between the two Corgis. Physically the Pembroke's ears are medium sized and taper slightly to a rounded point, while the Cardigan's ears are more rounded at the tip. The Cardigan Welsh Corgi is slightly larger and more heavily built than the Pembroke. Generally the Pembroke's feet point directly forward while the Cardigan has a more bowed front, much like that of the Basset Hound, and the feet point outward to some degree. The Pembroke is the more extroverted of the two, while the Cardigan is friendly but more reserved with strangers. The most obvious difference is that the Pembroke has natural bob or docked tail whereas the Cardigan has a full-length tail.

taught by its master before it understands what it may and may not do. Some breeds can be considered 'pushovers' in that they seem continually ready, willing and able to respond to their owner's commands. A Corgi not only has to know that you are serious about what you ask it to do but he also may have to think on it a bit as well.

The bottom line to all this is that your Cardigan will depend wholly and entirely upon you for everything it needs. If you are not ready to accept that responsibility, you are not ready to own a Cardi. It will only result in sheer drudgery and frustration for you, and an unhappy situation for the dog.

ARE YOU READY FOR A CARDIGAN?

Failure to understand the amount of time and consideration that a well-cared-for dog requires is one

then immediately insisting that it be let in.

Puppies experience just as many of the aches and pains and sniffles as the human child does on the way to maturity. Albeit over a shorter time span, but, even at that, all too often the many needs are not realistically considered before adding a dog to one's household. It takes time and planning to fulfil the day-to-day needs of a dog, whether puppy or fully-grown adult. This says nothing of the time required for the many lessons a Corgi must be

Rachel Stoltzman, age five, with her Cardi, Libbie, age nine months. Cardis and children can develop a special relationship based on trust and clean fun!

of the primary reasons for the number of unwanted canines that end their lives in animal shelters. Given proper consideration beforehand, the purchase of a dog can bring many years of companionship and comfort as well as unconditional love and devotion that no other animal can match. Before any person brings a dog into his home, he should give very serious consideration to three extremely important questions:

HERDING THE CHILDREN
There is no doubt that one of the most endearing traits of the Cardigan is its devotion to its owners. This is particularly so in regard to the children of the family. The Cardigan raised with children is as much their protector as it is their playmate—calling upon its herding heritage to keep the children shielded from danger.

Not naturally aquatic, Cardigans will do almost anything to spend time with their favourite children.

owning a new dog has worn off that must be considered.

In many active families, the ultimate responsibility for the family dog often falls on one person. Who will this person be? Can he really handle and does he really want more duties than he already has?

1. *Does the person who will ultimately be responsible for the dog's day-to-day care really want a dog?*
    The children may desperately want a dog; however, will they be doing more than just playing with the dog once it arrives? Pet care can be an excellent way to teach children responsibility, but it should not be forgotten that, in their enthusiasm to have a puppy, children are apt to promise almost anything. It is what will happen after the novelty of

SAVE THE 'WALES'
The Corgi breeds' debut as show dogs was less than auspicious and it is to the credit of those who championed the cause of the little working dogs from Wales that the two breeds survived at all. When the highly respected British dog man George Raper first laid eyes on the Corgis at a show, his only comment was said to be, 'Drown the lot!'

2. Does the lifestyle and schedule of the household lend itself to the demands of proper dog care?

There must always be someone available to see to a dog's basic needs: feeding, exercise, coat care, access to the outdoors when required and so on. If you or your family is gone from morning to night or if you travel frequently and are away from home for long periods of time, the dog still must be cared for. Will someone willingly be present to do so? Are you prepared to pay the costs of frequent boarding for your dog while you are gone?

HEEL, BOY!

High-energy children that are running and being noisy when outdoors playing can easily awaken the herding instinct in an untrained or uncontrolled Corgi. When this happens, the Cardi may dash off after the children, attempting to herd them or even attempting to nip at their heels. This can be both frightening and traumatic to the young child, who may be inclined to scream or cry and run even faster, further stimulating the herding instinct. This is a scenario that can be easily avoided by keeping your Corgi on leash.

DEVOTED WORKER

The Cardigan Welsh Corgi's history details all the mental and physical characteristics that served to produce both a hard-working, efficient herding dog and a fine household companion. Generations of selection on that basis give us a dog that is happiest when given a job to do that can be performed for those he loves.

3. Is the Cardigan Welsh Corgi suitable for the individual or household?

Corgis are wonderful with well-behaved children, but, on the other hand, no dog should be expected to tolerate abuse just because the child knows no better.

At the same time, an enthusiastic Cardi puppy or adult can unintentionally knock down and injure the toddler in a playful moment.

In addition to these three major questions regarding dog ownership, the prospective dog owner should strongly consider the specific peculiarities of his or her own lifestyle and household. All of this applies whether the household is made up of a single individual or a large family. Everyone involved must realise that the new dog will not understand the household routine and must be taught everything it needs to know and do. This takes time and patience and often the most important lessons for the new dog to learn will take the longest for it to absorb.

WHY A PURE-BRED?

There is no difference between the love, devotion and companionship that a mixed-breed dog and a pure-bred dog can give its owner. There are, however, some aspects of suitability that can best be fulfilled by the pure-bred dog.

Not all puppies will grow up to be particularly attractive adults or they may appeal only to someone with very exotic tastes. If your picture of the ideal dog is a Greyhound, a Cardigan is not going to live up to that ideal, nor will the Great Dane fit into life in a flat as easily as a Cardigan or another smaller breed.

Predicting what a mixed-breed puppy will look like at maturity is well nigh impossible. Size, length of hair and temperament can change drastically between puppyhood and adulthood and may be not at all what the owner had hoped. Then what happens to the dog?

In buying a well-bred Cardigan puppy, the purchaser will have a very good idea of what the dog will look like and how it will behave as an adult. Like all pure-bred dog breeds, the Cardigan Welsh Corgi has been bred for generations to meet specifications of conformation and temperament. This does not mean that the Cardigan breed is the result of a giant 'cookie cutter.' Naturally, there are differences within breeds just as there are differences from human to human. At the same time, the general character of a specific breed is far more predictable than that of a dog of unknown parentage.

When choosing a puppy, one must have the adult dog in mind because the little fellow is going to be an adult much longer than it ever was a puppy. The eventual size and temperament of the adult dog are what must fit the owner's lifestyle and aesthetic standards. The Cardigan's compact size makes him adaptable to smaller living spaces, but he will need sufficient opportunity to exercise, whether living in a flat or on a farm.

A fastidious housekeeper may well have second thoughts when trying to accommodate a very large breed that slobbers or one that casts coat all year around. It may come as a surprise to some, but all dogs shed to some degree.

A lovely litter of Cardis almost ready for leaving to their new homes. Know what you are looking for in a Cardi puppy before you commit to the purchase.

Shorter hair is less noticeable on clothing and furniture but far more difficult to pick up with a vacuum or brush than long hair. Corgis shed twice a year; if you don't brush thoroughly during the shedding periods, you will find the hair on your clothing and all over your furniture and floors. Brushing out the old hair helps the moulting process and minimises the amount of dog hair around the home.

With pure-bred dogs, you are reasonably assured of selecting a dog compatible with your lifestyle. Even at that, you must spend some time with adult Cardigan Corgis before you buy one in order to truly appreciate what life with one might be like in your own household.

The initial purchase price of a pure-bred Cardigan could easily be a significant investment for the owner, but a pure-bred Corgi costs no more to maintain than a mixed breed. If the cost of having exactly the kind of dog you want and are proud to own is amortised over the number of years during which you will enjoy its company, you will have to admit that the initial cost becomes far less consequential.

CAN A CARDIGAN BE A GOOD HOUSE DOG?

A Cardigan is entirely capable of being anyone's best friend and household companion, but, as is the case in any good relationship, both parties must be compatible. Corgis were bred to work. At no time in either breed's developmental history was any attempt made to make the Corgi a lap dog or boudoir companion. A Corgi best belongs to someone who will not begrudge the time it takes to give the dog some work to do. Corgis must be given their daily duties or they may well use up their excess time by inventing things to do. What your Cardigan decides to do on its own might be gnawing on the legs of your best antique table, excavating your newly planted flower bed or herding your neighbour's cat.

Retrieving comes naturally to Corgis—putting this talent to use in having your Cardigan bring you the morning paper or in playing some cleverly devised game is 'work' that he will enjoy. Although obedience work might mean one thing to you, to a Corgi it could mean the difference between boredom and a job that it looks forward to performing well.

All of this is not to indicate that your Cardigan is an incessantly busy or neurotic little fellow. On the contrary, your dog will enjoy those quiet moments sitting next to you while you read or listen to music as much as you

DID YOU KNOW?

Challenge keeps the Cardi vital and youthful even into old age. Agility, obedience and tracking provide excellent venues in which the breed is able to prove its ability. Kennel Club records reveal that the Cardigan stands proudly among all breeds when it comes to employing brain power.

do. However, your Cardi does need directed activity to take the edge off his inherited ability to put in a full day's work.

Corgis are lovers of routine and once they learn the household routine they are usually one step ahead of their owners in following it. However, while routine is appreciated, monotony is not. Approach training your Cardigan with variety and enthusiasm. Cardis learn quickly. Repeating a lesson over and over will bore the average Cardi and it will rebel. 'Not,' as some Corgi owners say, 'to be spiteful, but just to put a slightly different slant on what it is doing!'

The breed is short of coat and long on endurance, reasonably tolerant of both heat and cold. They love their homes and have no great urge to roam, especially if there is plenty to do on home ground. However, the Cardigan is curious and, lacking a fenced garden, he or she might decide to check out the 'other side of the mountain' on occasion.

The Corgi can be trained to do just about anything a dog is capable of doing, particularly if the task includes agility and enthusiasm. The only thing a Corgi is short on is legs.

DECIDING WHO IS BOSS
The Cardigan Corgi is definitely a breed with a highly developed

sense of curiosity and a mind of its own. If your Cardi is involved in exploring or in tracking down some real or imagined mystery creature, something like answering your first call may not be nearly as enticing to him.

Owners who have been negligent in making their Cardigans understand who makes all the rules and that the rules must always be obeyed may find themselves left out of decision-making entirely. If you do not provide the requisite leadership, your Cardi will let you know in no uncertain terms that it is entirely capable of providing that leadership for itself.

With all that said, if a prospective owner is willing to take on the responsibilities required of a Cardigan owner, there are few breeds that can provide more devotion and companionship than this one. The Cardigan lives to be with its owner, and since it is a breed that is just about the right size to go anywhere—not too large and not too small—it is afforded many opportunities to go places and do things with its human companions.

MALE OR FEMALE?

While some people may have personal preferences as to the sex of their dog, we can honestly say that both male and female Cardigans make equally good

DOGS, DOGS, GOOD FOR YOUR HEART!

People usually purchase dogs for companionship, but studies show that dogs can help to improve their owners' health and level of activity, as well as lower a human's risk of coronary heart disease. Without even realising it, when a person puts time into exercising, grooming and feeding a dog, he also puts more time into his own personal health care. Dog owners establish more routine schedules for their dogs to follow, which can have positive effects on a human's health. Dogs also teach us patience, offer unconditional love and provide the joy of having a furry friend to pet!

companions and are equal in their trainability and affection. The decision of gender will have more to do with the lifestyle and ultimate plans of the owner than with differences between the sexes in the breed.

A male may take a bit longer to grow up than a female, and may experience a brief bashful period on his way to maturity. However, some owners say that given a choice of only one dog, male or female, they would probably choose a male in that males are unusually sweet and cooperative.

The male Cardigan is normally larger and heavier boned than the female, and does present one problem that the prospective buyer should consider. While both the male and the female must be trained not to urinate in the home, the male of any breed of dog has a natural instinct to lift his leg and urinate on objects to establish and 'mark' his territory. The degree of effort that must be invested in training the male not to do this varies with the individual dog. This habit becomes increasingly more difficult to correct with the number of times a male dog is used for breeding; the mating act increases his need and desire to mark his territory.

The female is not entirely problem-free. She will have her semi-annual, and sometimes burdensome, heat cycle after she is eight or nine months old. At these times she must be confined so that she will not soil her surroundings, and she must also be closely watched to prevent male dogs from gaining access to her or she will become pregnant.

ALTERING

Having the pet Cardigan 'altered' can effectively eliminate both of these sexually associated problems. Spaying the female and neutering the male will not change the personality of your pet and will avoid many problems. Neutering the male Corgi can reduce, if not entirely eliminate, its desire to pursue a neighbour-hood female that shows signs of an impending romantic attitude.

DO YOU WANT TO LIVE LONGER?

If you like to volunteer, it is wonderful if you can take your dog to a nursing home once a week for several hours. The elderly community loves to have a dog with which to visit, and often your dog will bring a bit of companionship to someone who is lonely or somewhat detached from the world. You will be not only bringing happiness to someone else but also keeping your dog busy—and we haven't even mentioned the fact that it has been discovered that volunteering helps to increase your own longevity!

Neutering and spaying also precludes the possibility of your Cardigan's adding to the pet-overpopulation problem that concerns environmentalists world-wide. Altering also reduces the risk of mammary cancer in the female and testicular cancer in the male.

HEALTH CONCERNS

It is not the least bit unusual to have the well-cared-for Cardigan Corgi live to be 12 to 14 years of age, still acting hale and hearty. However, like with most other breeds of domesticated dog, the Cardigan has its share of hereditary problems; fortunately, the problems are relatively few.

The diseases described here are not rampant in the breed and are fully understood by respected breeders. They are breed problems, however, that should be discussed with the breeder from whom you purchase your dog.

BACK AND JOINT PROBLEMS

Because of their long backs and short-legged conformation, the Cardigan is susceptible to back and joint problems. Owners should limit or even eliminate the opportunities for puppies and young dogs to leap on and off chairs or manoeuvre stairs. High-impact games and exercises should be avoided until a Corgi is at least a year old.

RUPTURED DISC SYNDROME

Although some attribute ruptured disc syndrome entirely to the fact that the Cardigan Corgi is a long-backed breed, it is worthwhile to note that this is not entirely the case. There are a number of short-backed breeds that are also affected by this same

TAKING CARE

Science is showing that as people take care of their pets, the pets are taking care of their owners. A study in 1998, published in the *American Journal of Cardiology*, found that having a pet can prolong his owner's life. Pet owners generally have lower blood pressure, and pets help their owners to relax and keep more physically fit. It was also found that pets help to keep the elderly connected to their community.

problem while many other long-backed breeds are not. Thus, it appears this is more likely a matter of individual sensitivity and that certain bloodlines are more prone to this sensitivity than others.

In short, the ruptured disc syndrome is that in which the sponge-like disc that acts as a cushion between the spinal vertebrae ruptures. The pressure of this ruptured disc against the spinal column causes extreme pain and, in some cases, partial or complete paralysis of the hindquarters.

Normal activity in an adult, including jumping off furniture, going up and down stairs, etc., will not cause discs to rupture unless the dog is prone to the condition in the first place. Again, this is looked upon as a condition that can be more or less prevalent in some lines and definitely bears being discussed with the breeder of the puppy you are considering.

HIP DYSPLASIA

Hip dysplasia, commonly referred to as 'HD,' is a developmental disease of the hip joint in which one or both hip joints of the affected dog have abnormal contours. A dog might show tenderness in the hip, walk with a limp or swaying gait or experience difficulty getting up. Symptoms vary from

mild temporary lameness to severe crippling in extreme cases. Treatment may require surgery. Even though hip dysplasia is not rampant in the Corgi breeds, enough cases have been reported to merit asking the breeder of your puppy what testing he has done in respect to the problem.

EYE PROBLEMS

The Cardigan Corgi experiences progressive retinal atrophy (PRA) and secondary glaucoma to a degree that screening has become necessary. Conscientious breeders test all of their breeding stock and do not use animals in their breeding programmes that carry the genes for these conditions.

The condition commonly referred to as 'PRA' is the most common eye disease affecting the Cardigan. It is a degenerative disease of the retinal cells of the eye that progresses to blindness. It usually occurs later in life, typically in Corgis more than six years old.

Secondary glaucoma is not entirely uncommon. Glaucoma involves increased pressure within the eye. When the fluid created by this pressure is unable to escape from the eye, the eyeball becomes swollen and painful. This is a congenital condition, but it seldom appears until the dog has fully matured.

DO YOU KNOW ABOUT HIP DYSPLASIA?

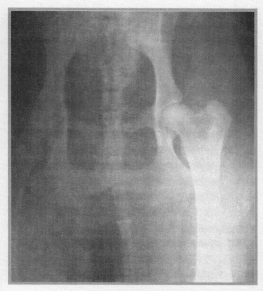

X-ray of a dog with 'Good' hips.

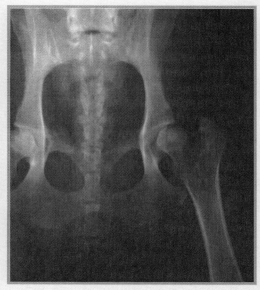

X-ray of a dog with 'Moderate' dysplastic hips.

Hip dysplasia is a fairly common condition found in pure-bred dogs. When a dog has hip dysplasia, its hind leg has an incorrectly formed hip joint. By constant use of the hip joint, it becomes more and more loose, wears abnormally and may become arthritic.

Hip dysplasia can only be confirmed with an x-ray, but certain symptoms may indicate a problem. Your dog may have a hip dysplasia problem if it walks in a peculiar manner, hops instead of smoothly runs, uses its hind legs in unison (to keep the pressure off the weak joint), has trouble getting up from a prone position or always sits with both legs together on one side of its body.

As the dog matures, it may adapt well to life with a bad hip, but in a few years the arthritis develops and many dogs with hip dysplasia become cripples.

Hip dysplasia is considered an inherited disease and only can be diagnosed definitively when the dog is two years old. Some experts claim that a special diet might help your puppy outgrow the bad hip, but the usual treatments are surgical. The removal of the pectineus muscle, the removal of the round part of the femur, reconstructing the pelvis and replacing the hip with an artificial one are all surgical interventions that are expensive, but they are usually very successful. Follow the advice of your veterinary surgeon.

Breed Standard for the
CARDIGAN WELSH CORGI

A Cardigan Welsh Corgi of the proper shape, balance and proportion creates a picture of a tough little working dog that is fit and able to perform his duties for the whole day long if necessary. The question that arises, however, is what tells us if a Cardigan does, in fact, have the right structure and shape, balance and proportion?

The answers to all these are found in The Kennel Club's breed standard. A breed standard is a detailed and accurate description of the ideal specimen of a given breed. A standard describes the dog physically—listing all of a breed's anatomical parts and telling how those parts should look. The standard also describes the breed's temperament and how

The breed standard describes the appearance of the breed as well as its movement. Judges observe the Cardigan's gait in the show ring to ensure that it is free and active with good forward reaching in the front and thrusting in the rear.

it should move about.

The standard is the blueprint that breeders use to fashion their breeding programmes. The goal, of course, is to move one step closer to that ever-elusive picture of perfection with each succeeding generation. A breed standard also is what dog show judges use to determine which of the dogs being shown compares most favourably to what is required of its given breed.

It should be understood that what the standard describes is the perfect dog of a given breed. In nature, nothing is absolutely perfect. Thus, the breeder and the judge are looking for the dog that, in their opinions, has 'most of the best.' How each individual person interprets the standard will always vary somewhat, but there is usually little disagreement when a dog comes along that truly has most of what the breed standard actually asks for. No dog will have it all.

Although it takes many years to fully understand the implications of a breed standard, it behooves the prospective owner of any breed to familiarise himself with requirements therein. This will enable the person who wishes to own a dog of that breed to be able to have a good idea of what a representative specimen should look and act like.

Although some observers see the main difference between the

BREEDING CONSIDERATIONS

The decision to breed your dog is one that must be considered carefully and researched thoroughly before moving into action. Some people believe that breeding will make their bitches happier or that it is an easy way to make money. Unfortunately, indiscriminate breeding only worsens the rampant problem of pet overpopulation, as well as putting a considerable dent in your pocketbook. As for the bitch, the entire process from mating through whelping is not an easy one and puts your pet under considerable stress. Last, but not least, consider whether or not you have the means to care for an entire litter of pups. Without a reputation in the field, your attempts to sell the pups may be unsuccessful.

Cardigan and Pembroke Welsh Corgis as primarily one of tails— with the Cardigan's having the long brush tail and the Pembroke's

The Cardi is a tough, mobile dog, long and low to the ground, with large erect ears. This dog possesses the breed's unique brindle pattern.

having no tail—the respective enthusiasts of each breed tell a much different *tale*. It is important to understand that the two Corgis are not two variations or varieties of the same breed, but two separate and distinct breeds.

Cardigan enthusiasts will quickly state that their breed has an entirely different origin than the Pembroke, with theirs descending from the ancient Teckel, a low-slung and dwarf-legged European dog. Clearly the physical differences between the two extend far beyond tail length.

THE KENNEL CLUB BREED STANDARD FOR THE WELSH CORGI (CARDIGAN)

General Appearance: Sturdy, tough, mobile, capable of endurance. Long in proportion to

height, terminating in fox-like brush, set in line with body.

Characteristics: Alert, active and intelligent.

Temperament: Alert, intelligent, steady, not shy or aggressive.

Head and Skull: Head foxy in shape and appearance, skull wide and flat between ears tapering towards eyes above which it is slightly domed. Moderate stop. Length of foreface in proportion to head 3 to 5, muzzle tapering moderately towards nose which projects slightly and in no sense blunt. Under-jaw clean cut. Strong but without prominence. Nose black.

Eyes: Medium size, clear, giving kindly, alert but watchful expression. Rather widely set with corners clearly defined. Preferably dark, to blend with coat, rims dark. One or both eyes pale blue, blue or blue flecked, permissible only in blue merles.

Ears: Erect, proportionately rather large to size of dog. Tips slightly rounded, moderately wide at base and set about 8 cms (3.5 ins) apart. Carried so that tips are slightly wide of straight line drawn from tip of nose through centre of eyes, and set well back so that they can be laid flat along neck.

Mouth: Teeth strong, with scissor bite, i.e. upper teeth closely overlapping lower teeth and set square to jaws.

Neck: Muscular, well developed, in proportion to dog's build, fitting into well sloping shoulders.

Forequarters: Shoulders well laid, angulated at approximately 90 degrees to upper arm; muscular, elbows close to sides. Strong bone carried down to feet. Legs short but body well clear of the ground, forearms slightly bowed to mould around the chest. Feet turned slightly outwards.

Body: Chest moderately broad with prominent breast bone. Body fairly long and strong, with deep brisket, well sprung ribs. Clearly defined waist. Topline level.

Pembroke Welsh Corgi head study, showing the breed's smaller prick ears, set closer together.

Cardigan Welsh Corgi head study, showing large, flared ears and slightly longer muzzle.

Pembroke Welsh Corgi body study, more compact, square, with straighter front and no tail.

Cardigan Welsh Corgi, longer in body, with properly angulated shoulders and fox-brush tail.

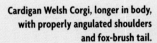

Cardigan Welsh Corgi, ideal body in the breed's unique brindle coloration.

Faulty Cardigan body, lacking angulation, with overly long legs; chest lacking deth; poor topline; and poor tailset and carriage.

Hindquarters: Strong, well angulated and aligned with muscular thighs and second thighs, strong bone carried down to feet, legs short when standing, hocks vertical when viewed from side and rear.

Feet: Round, tight, rather large and well padded. All dewclaws to be removed.

Tail: Like a fox's brush, set in line with the body and moderately long (to touch or nearly touch ground). Carried low when standing but may be lifted a little above body when moving, not curled over back.

Gait/Movement: Free and active, elbows sitting close to sides, neither loose nor tied. Forelegs reaching well forward without too much lift, in unison with thrusting action of hindlegs.

Coat: Short or medium of hard texture. Weather-proof, with good undercoat. Preferably straight.

Colour: Any colour, with or without white markings, but white should not predominate.

Size: Height: ideal 30 cms (12 ins) at shoulder. Weight in proportion to size with overall balance the prime consideration.

Faults: Any departure from the foregoing points should be considered a fault and the seriousness with which the fault should be regarded should be in exact proportion to its degree.

Note: Male animals should have two apparently normal testicles fully descended into the scrotum.

Desirable Cardigan head, in blue merle pattern.

BREEDER'S BLUEPRINT

If you are considering breeding your bitch, it is very important that you are familiar with the breed standard. Reputable breeders breed with the intention of producing dogs that are as close as possible to the standard and that contribute to the advancement of the breed. Study the standard for both physical appearance and temperament, and make certain your bitch and your chosen stud dog measure up.

HOW TO SELECT A CARDIGAN PUPPY

Your Cardigan will live with you for many years. Therefore, it is extremely important that the dog comes from a source where physical and mental soundness are primary considerations in the breeding programme, usually the result of careful breeding over a period of many years.

There may be a bit of a problem in locating a Cardigan Corgi breeder, as the breed is numerically small and Cardigan breeders do not breed often. They are inclined to have long waiting

PUPPY APPEARANCE
Your puppy should have a well-fed appearance but not a distended abdomen, which may indicate worms or incorrect feeding, or both. The body should be firm, with a solid feel. The skin of the abdomen should be pale pink and clean, without signs of scratching or rash. Check the hind legs to make certain that dewclaws were removed, if any were present at birth.

lists for the puppies that are available. Those who own Cardigans, however, feel that the breed is well worth the wait and can refer you to good breeders. The Kennel Club also is able to recommend breeders of quality Cardigans, as can any local all-breed club or Corgi club.

Visiting a breeder's home or kennel gives the buyer the distinct advantage of seeing the parents, or at least the mother, of the puppies that are available. The breeder normally will have other relatives of the puppy you are interested in on the premises as well.

Experienced breeders know which hereditary problems exist

The days of puppyhood will fly by! Don't forgot to enjoy your puppy and to stop to smell the flowers—he won't!

in the breed and will be happy to discuss them with you. Practically all breeds are subject to inherited ailments and Corgis are no exception. Beware of breeders who tell you that their dogs are not susceptible to inherited diseases or potential problems. We do not mean to imply that all Corgis are afflicted with genetic problems, but a reliable breeder will give you the information you are entitled to know regarding the individual you are considering.

Inspect the environment in which the dogs are raised. Cleanliness is as important to producing good stock as are good pedigrees. The time you spend in researching and inspecting the kennel and the adult dogs it houses may well save you a great deal of money and heartache in the years to come.

A good question to ask the breeder of the puppy you are considering is why he or she breeds Cardis. A responsible breeder will have definite reasons for having produced a litter. The

PUPPY SELECTION
Your selection of a good puppy can be determined by your needs. A show potential or a good pet? It is your choice. Every puppy, however, should be of good temperament. Although show-quality puppies are bred and raised with emphasis on physical conformation, responsible breeders strive for equally good temperament. Do not buy from a breeder who concentrates solely on physical beauty at the expense of personality.

DID YOU KNOW?
You should not even think about buying a puppy that looks sick, undernourished, overly frightened or nervous. Sometimes a timid puppy will warm up to you after a 30-minute 'let's-get-acquainted' session.

reasons could be varied, because the Cardigan is a very adaptable breed that is suitable for many purposes, but if you suspect the breeder you are speaking to breeds only to sell puppies, we would suggest you look elsewhere.

Socialisation for the pups is critical for all breeds. The ideal situation is where the Cardi puppies are with their dam when you inspect them. The dam's demeanour will strongly reflect the personality of the pups.

WHAT TO LOOK FOR IN A PUP

Above all, the Cardi puppy you buy should be a happy, playful extrovert. Never select a puppy that appears sickly because you feel sorry for it and feel you will be able to nurse it back to good health. Well-bred Cardigan puppies with positive temperaments are not afraid of strangers. You should not settle for anything less. Under normal circumstances, you will have the whole litter in your lap if you kneel and call them to you.

Check inside the puppy's ears. They should be pink and clean. Any odour or dark discharge could indicate ear mites, which in turn would indicate poor maintenance. The inside of the puppy's mouth and gums should be pink, and the teeth should be clean and white. There should be no malformation of the mouth or jaw. The eyes should be clear and bright. Again, be aware of any signs of discharge. The nose of a Cardigan puppy should never be crusted or running.

Corgi puppies should feel compact and substantial to the touch. They should not be bony and undernourished, nor should they be bloated; a taut and bloated abdomen is usually a sign of worms. A rounded puppy belly is normal. Coughing or signs of diarrhoea are danger signals as are skin eruptions.

Conformation and physical structure is important, even at an early age, and for both potential show puppies and pet puppies. The movement should be free and easy. Limping or stumbling could easily mean life-long problems. While a pet puppy does not need perfect conformation by show ring standards, he needs to be put together properly to grow up to be a healthy adult.

If you have been reading and doing your research, you can expect the Cardi puppy to look much like a miniaturised version of an adult. The Cardigan Corgi will achieve practically all of its growth by six to eight months, but is not fully mature until about three years of age.

The puppy coat will be softer and finer than the adult coat, but the hair should never be long or fluffy. Ears may not yet be standing or one ear may be up and the other down. If the ears aren't standing, simply hold the puppy on its back in your two hands and tilt its head downward. The ears will lie back and this will give you a picture of what the

DOCUMENTATION

Two important documents you will get from the breeder are the pup's pedigree and registration certificate. The breeder should register the litter and each pup with The Kennel Club, and it is necessary for you to have the paperwork if you plan on showing or breeding in the future.

Make sure you know the breeder's intentions on which type of registration he will obtain for the pup. There are limited registrations which may prohibit the dog from being shown, bred or competing in non-conformation trials such as Working or Agility if the breeder feels that the pup is not of sufficient quality to do so. There is also a type of registration that will permit the dog in non-conformation competition only.

On the reverse side of the registration certificate, the new owner can find the transfer section, which must be signed by the breeder.

INSURANCE

Many good breeders will offer you insurance with your new puppy, which is an excellent idea. The first few weeks of insurance will probably be covered free of charge or with only minimal cost, allowing you to take up the policy when this expires. If you own a pet dog, it is sensible to take out such a policy as veterinary fees can be high, although routine vaccinations and boosters are not covered. Look carefully at the many options open to you before deciding which suits you best.

puppy will look like when his ears stand on their own. Ears may seem a bit large at this early stage but, more often than not, the puppy will grow into them.

SHOW DOG OR COMPANION?
If you want to be assured of a dog of real show quality, then finding a puppy that comes from winning

most any breeder can say about an eight-week-old Cardigan puppy is that it has or does not have 'show potential.'

If the excitement and pride of owning a winning show dog appeals to you, we strongly urge you to seek out a successful breeder who has a record of having produced winning dogs through the years. As stated, it is extremely difficult, if not impossible, to predict what an eight-week-old puppy will look like as an adult. An experienced breeder, however, will know whether a young puppy has potential.

WHERE TO BEGIN?

If you are convinced that the Cardigan Welsh Corgi is the ideal dog for you, it's time to begin your search. You should enquire about breeders in your area who enjoy a good reputation in the breed. You are looking for an established

PUPPY PERSONALITY

When a litter becomes available to you, choosing a pup out of all those adorable faces will not be an easy task! Sound temperament is of utmost importance, but each pup has its own personality and some may be better suited to you than others. A feisty, independent pup will do well in a home with older children and adults, while quiet, shy puppies will thrive in a home with minimal noise and distractions. Your breeder knows the pups best and should be able to guide you in the right direction.

stock becomes a major consideration. Also, the older the puppy is at the time of selection, the more likely you will know how good the dog will be at maturity. The

BOY OR GIRL?

An important consideration to be discussed is the sex of your puppy. For a family companion, a bitch may be the better choice, considering the female's inbred concern for all young creatures and her accompanying tolerance and patience. It is always advisable to spay a pet bitch, which may guarantee her a longer life.

ARE YOU A FIT OWNER?

If the breeder from whom you are buying a puppy asks you a lot of personal questions, do not be insulted. Such a breeder wants to be sure that you will be a fit provider for his puppy.

INHERIT THE MIND

In order to know whether or not a puppy will fit into your lifestyle, you need to assess his personality. A good way to do this is to interact with his parents. Your pup inherits not only his appearance but also his personality and temperament from the sire and dam. If the parents are fearful or overly aggressive, these same traits may likely show up in your puppy.

breeder with outstanding dog ethics and a strong commitment to the breed. New owners should have as many questions as they have doubts. An established breeder is indeed the one to answer your four million questions and make you comfortable with your choice of the Cardigan Welsh Corgi. An established breeder will sell you a puppy at a fair price if, and only if, the breeder determines that you are a suitable, worthy owner of his dogs. An established breeder can be relied upon for advice, no matter what time of day or night. A reputable breeder will accept a puppy back, without questions, should you decide that this is not the right dog for you.

When choosing a breeder, reputation is much more important than convenience of location. Do not be overly impressed by breeders who run brag advertisements in the presses about their stupendous champions. The real quality breeders are quiet and unassuming. You hear about them

'YOU BETTER SHOP AROUND!'

Finding a reputable breeder that sells healthy pups is very important, but make sure that the breeder you choose is not only someone you respect but also with whom you feel comfortable. Your breeder will be a resource long after you buy your puppy, and you must be able to call with reasonable questions without being made to feel like a pest! If you don't connect on a personal level, investigate some other breeders before making a final decision.

as much as any established breeder. The novice breeder isn't going to interrogate you and your family about your intentions with the puppy, the environment and training you can provide, etc. That breeder will be nowhere to be found when your poorly bred, badly adjusted four-pawed monster starts to growl and spit up at midnight or eat the family cat!

Choosing a breeder is an important first step in dog ownership. Fortunately, the majority of Cardigan Welsh Corgi breeders is devoted to the breed and its well-being. Potential owners are encouraged to attend dog shows (or trials) to see the Cardigans in action, to meet the owners and handlers firsthand and to get an idea of what Cardigans look like outside a photographer's lens. Provided you approach the handlers when they are not terribly busy with the dogs, most are more than willing to answer questions, recommend breeders and give advice.

Once you have contacted and met a breeder or two and made your choice about which breeder is best suited to your needs, it's time to visit the litter. Again, keep in mind that many top breeders have waiting lists. Sometimes new owners have to wait as long as two years for a puppy. If you are really committed to the breeder whom you've selected, then you

at the dog trials and shows, by word of mouth. You may be well advised to avoid the novice who lives only a few miles away. The local novice breeder, trying so hard to get rid of that first litter of puppies, is more than accommodating and anxious to sell you one. That breeder will charge you

will wait (and hope for an early arrival!). If not, you may have to resort to your second- or third-choice breeder. Don't be too anxious, however. If the breeder doesn't have a waiting list, or any customers, there is probably a good reason. It's no different than visiting a pub with no clientele. The better pubs and restaurants always have a waiting list—and it's usually worth the wait. Besides, isn't a puppy more important than a pint?

Since you are likely to be choosing a Cardigan Welsh Corgi as a pet dog and not a show dog, you simply should select a pup that is friendly and attractive. The average litter size ranges considerably, from three or four to as high as six or seven puppies.

The gender of your puppy is largely a matter of personal taste. Males tend to take a while longer to 'grow up' than females, but are very sweet and co-operative. The difference in size is noticeable, with the male being larger, but a male Cardigan is still a compact dog. Coloration is not a grave concern with this breed, though white cannot predominate in a show puppy.

Breeders commonly allow visitors to see the litter by around the fifth or sixth week, and puppies leave for their new homes between the eighth and tenth week. Breeders who permit their puppies to leave early are

PREPARING FOR PUP

Unfortunately, when a puppy is bought by someone who does not take into consideration the time and attention that dog ownership requires, it is the puppy who suffers when he is either abandoned or placed in a shelter by a frustrated owner. So all of the 'homework' you do in preparation for your pup's arrival will benefit you both. The more informed you are, the more you will know what to expect and the better equipped you will be to handle the ups and downs of raising a puppy. Hopefully, everyone in the household is willing to do his part in raising and caring for the pup. The anticipation of owning a dog often brings a lot of promises from excited family members: 'I will walk him every day,' 'I will feed him,' 'I will house-train him,' etc., but these things take time and effort, and promises can easily be forgotten once the novelty of the new pet has worn off.

more interested in your pounds than their puppies' well being. Puppies need to learn the rules of the pack from their dams, and most dams continue teaching the pups manners and dos and don'ts until around the eighth week. Breeders spend significant amounts of time with the Cardigan toddlers so that they are able to interact with the 'other species,' i.e. humans. Given the

DID YOU KNOW?

Breeders rarely release puppies until they are eight to ten weeks of age. This is an acceptable age for most breeds of dog, excepting toy breeds, which are not released until around 12 weeks, given their petite sizes. If a breeder has a puppy that is 12 weeks of age or older, it is likely well socialised and house-trained. Be sure that it is otherwise healthy before deciding to take it home.

long history that dogs and humans have, bonding between the two species is natural but must be nurtured. A well-bred, well-socialised Cardigan Welsh Corgi pup wants nothing more than to be near you and please you. Socialisation is the first and best way to encourage a proper, stable personality in puppies.

Always check the bite of your selected puppy to be sure that it is neither overshot nor undershot. This may not be too noticeable on a young puppy, but will become more evident as the pup matures.

COMMITMENT OF OWNERSHIP

After considering all of these factors, you have most likely already made some very important decisions about selecting your puppy. You have chosen the Cardigan Welsh Corgi as your breed, which means that you have decided which characteristics you want in a dog and what type of dog will best fit into your family and lifestyle. If you have selected a breeder, you have gone a step further—you have done your research and found a responsible, conscientious person who breeds quality Cardigan Welsh Corgis and who should be a reliable source of help as you and your puppy adjust to life together. If you have observed a litter in action, you have obtained a firsthand look at the dynamics of a puppy 'pack' and, thus, you should learn about each pup's individual personality—perhaps you have even found one that particularly appeals to you.

However, even if you have not yet found the Cardigan Welsh Corgi puppy of your dreams, observing pups will help you learn to recognise certain behaviour and to determine what a pup's behaviour indicates about his temperament. You will be able to pick out which pups are the leaders, which ones are less outgoing, which ones are confident, which ones are shy, playful, friendly, aggressive, etc. Equally as important, you will learn to recognise what a healthy pup should look and act like. All of these things will help you in your search, and when you find the Cardigan Welsh Corgi that was meant for you, you will know it!

Researching your breed, selecting a responsible breeder and observing as many pups as possible are all important steps on the way to dog ownership. It may seem like a lot of effort…and you have not even taken the pup home yet! Remember, though, you cannot be too careful when it comes to deciding on the type of dog you want and finding out about your prospective pup's background. Buying a puppy is not—or should not be—just another whimsical purchase. This is one instance in which you actually do get to choose your

YOUR SCHEDULE . . .
If you lead an erratic, unpredictable life, with daily or weekly changes in your work requirements, consider the problems of owning a puppy. The new puppy has to be fed regularly, socialised (loved, petted, handled, introduced to other people) and, most importantly, allowed to visit outdoors for toilet training. As the dog gets older, it can be more tolerant of deviations in its feeding and toilet relief.

own family! You may be thinking that buying a puppy should be fun—it should not be so serious and so much work. Keep in mind that your puppy is not a cuddly stuffed toy or decorative lawn ornament, but a creature that will become a real member of your family. You will come to realise that, while buying a puppy is a pleasurable and exciting endeavour, it is not something to be taken lightly. Relax...the fun will start when the pup comes home!

Always keep in mind that a puppy is nothing more than a baby in a furry disguise...a baby who is virtually helpless in a human world and who trusts his owner for fulfilment of his basic needs for survival. In addition to water and shelter, your pup needs care, protection, guidance and love. If you are not prepared to commit to this, then you are not prepared to own a dog.

Wait a minute, you say. How hard could this be? All of my neighbours own dogs and they seem to be doing just fine. Why should I have to worry about all of this? Well, you should not

QUALITY FOOD
The cost of food must be mentioned. All dogs need a good-quality food with an adequate supply of protein to develop their bones and muscles properly. Most dogs are not picky eaters but, unless fed properly, can quickly succumb to skin problems.

worry about it; in fact, you will probably find that once your Cardigan Welsh Corgi pup gets used to his new home, he will fall into his place in the family quite naturally. But it never hurts to emphasise the commitment of dog ownership. With some time and patience, it is really not too difficult to raise a curious and exuberant Cardi pup to be a well-adjusted and well-mannered adult dog—a dog that could be your most loyal friend.

PREPARING PUPPY'S PLACE IN YOUR HOME
Researching your breed and finding a breeder are only two aspects of the 'homework' you will have to do before taking your Cardigan puppy home. You will also have to prepare your home and family for the new addition. Much as you would prepare a nursery for a newborn baby, you will need to designate a place in your home that will be the puppy's own. How you prepare your home will depend on how much freedom the dog will be allowed. Whatever you decide, you must ensure that he has a place that he can 'call his own.'

When you bring your new puppy into your home, you are bringing him into what will become his home as well. Obviously, you did not buy a puppy so that he could take over your house, but in order for a puppy to grow into a stable, well-adjusted dog, he has to feel comfortable in his surroundings. Remember, he is leaving the warmth and security of his mother and littermates, as well as the familiarity of the only place he has ever known, so it is important to make his transition as easy as possible. By preparing a place in your home for the puppy, you are making him feel as welcome as possible in a strange new place. It should not take him long to get used to it, but the sudden shock of being transplanted is somewhat traumatic for a young pup. Imagine how a small child would feel in the same situation—that is how your puppy must be feeling. It is up to you to reassure him and to let him know, 'Little chap, you are going to like it here!'

WHAT YOU SHOULD BUY

CRATE

To someone unfamiliar with the use of crates in dog training, it may seem like punishment to shut a dog in a crate, but this is not the case at all. Although all breeders do not advocate crate training, more and more breeders and trainers are recommending crates as preferred tools for show puppies as well as pet puppies. Crates are not cruel—crates have many humane and highly effective uses in dog care and

FIRST MEAL AT HOME

You will probably start feeding your pup the same food that he has been getting from the breeder; the breeder should give you a few days' supply to start you off. Although you should not give your pup too many treats, you will want to have puppy treats on hand for coaxing, training, rewards, etc. Be careful, though, as a small pup's calorie requirements are relatively low and a few treats can add up to almost a full day's worth of calories without the required nutrition.

PHOTO COURTESY OF DOSKOCIL

training. For example, crate training is a very popular and very successful house-training method. A crate can keep your dog safe during travel and, perhaps most importantly, a crate provides your dog with a place of his own in your home. It serves as a 'doggie bedroom' of sorts—your Cardigan Welsh Corgi can curl up in his crate when he wants to sleep or when he just needs a break. Many dogs sleep in their crates overnight. With soft bedding and his favourite toy, a crate becomes a cosy pseudo-den for your dog. Like his ancestors, he too will seek out the comfort and retreat of a den—you just happen to be providing him with something a little more luxurious than what his early ancestors enjoyed.

As far as purchasing a crate, the type that you buy is up to you. It will most likely be one of the two most popular types: wire or fibreglass. There are advantages and disadvantages to each type. For example, a wire crate is more open, allowing the air to flow through and affording the dog a view of what is going on around him, while a fibreglass crate is sturdier. Both can double as travel crates, providing protection for the dog. The size of the crate is another thing to consider. Puppies do not stay puppies forever—in fact, sometimes it seems as if they grow right before your eyes. A tiny crate may be fine for a very young Cardigan Welsh Corgi pup, but it will not do him much good for long! Unless you have the money and the inclination to buy a new crate every time your pup has a growth spurt, it is better to get one that will accommodate your dog both as a pup and at full size. Look for a crate that is approximately 32 inches (81 cms) long by 22 inches (56 cms) wide by 23 inches (58 cms) high; this will be the ideal size to accommodate the average Cardigan Corgi through adulthood.

BEDDING

Veterinary bedding in the dog's crate will help the dog feel more at home and you may also like to pop in a small blanket. This will take the place of the leaves, twigs, etc., that the pup would use in the wild to make a den; the pup can make his own 'burrow' in the crate. Although your pup is far removed from his den-making ancestors, the denning instinct is still a part of his genetic makeup. Second, until you take your pup home, he has been sleeping amid the warmth of his mother and littermates, and while a blanket is not the same as a warm, breathing body, it still provides heat and something with which to snuggle. You will want to wash your pup's bedding frequently in case he has an accident in his crate, and replace or remove any blanket that becomes ragged and starts to fall apart.

TOYS

Toys are a must for dogs of all ages, especially for curious playful pups. Puppies are the 'children' of the dog world, and what child does not love toys? Chew toys provide enjoyment for both dog and owner—your dog will enjoy playing with his favourite toys, while you will enjoy the fact that they distract him from your expensive shoes and leather sofa. Puppies love to chew; in fact, chewing is a

CRATE TRAINING TIPS

During crate training, you should partition off the section of the crate in which the pup stays. If he is given too big an area, this will hinder your training efforts. Crate training is based on the fact that a dog does not like to soil his sleeping quarters, so it is ineffective to keep a pup in a crate that is so big that he can eliminate in one end and get far enough away from it to sleep. Also, you want to make the crate den-like for the pup. Blankets and a favourite toy will make the crate cosy for the small pup; as he grows, you may want to evict some of his 'roommates' to make more room.

It will take some coaxing at first, but be patient. Given some time to get used to it, your pup will adapt to his new home-within-a-home quite nicely.

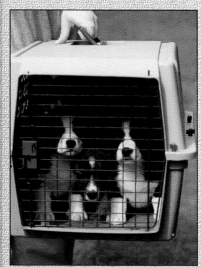

TOYS, TOYS, TOYS!

With a big variety of dog toys available, and so many that look like they would be a lot of fun for a dog, be careful in your selection. It is amazing what a set of puppy teeth can do to an innocent-looking toy, so, obviously, safety is a major consideration. Be sure to choose the most durable products that you can find. Hard nylon bones and toys are a safe bet, and many of them are offered in different scents and flavours that will be sure to capture your dog's attention. It is always fun to play a game of catch with your dog, and there are balls and flying discs that are specially made to withstand dog teeth.

physical need for pups as they are teething, and everything looks appetising! The full range of your possessions—from old tea towel to Oriental carpet—are fair game in the eyes of a teething pup. Puppies are not all that discerning when it comes to finding something to literally 'sink their teeth into'—everything tastes great!

Cardigan Welsh Corgi puppies are fairly aggressive chewers and only the hardest, strongest toys should be offered to them. Breeders advise owners to resist stuffed toys, because they can become de-stuffed in no time. The overly excited pup may ingest the stuffing, which is neither digestible nor nutritious.

Similarly, squeaky toys are quite popular, but must be avoided for the Cardigan. Perhaps a squeaky toy can be used as an aid in training, but not for free play. If a pup 'disembowels' one of these, the small plastic squeaker inside can be dangerous if swallowed. Monitor the condition of all your pup's toys carefully and get rid of any that have been chewed to the point of becoming potentially dangerous.

Be careful of natural bones, which have a tendency to splinter into sharp, dangerous pieces. Also be careful of rawhide, which can turn into pieces that are easy to swallow and become a mushy mess on your carpet.

LEAD

A nylon lead is probably the best option as it is the most resistant to puppy teeth should your pup take a liking to chewing on his lead. Of course, this is a habit that should be nipped in the bud, but if your pup likes to chew on his lead he has a very slim chance of being able to chew through the strong nylon. Nylon leads are also lightweight, which is good for a young Cardigan Welsh Corgi who is just getting used to the idea of walking on a lead. For everyday walking and safety purposes, the nylon lead is a good choice. As your pup grows up and gets used to walking on the lead, you may want to purchase a flexible lead. These leads allow you to extend the length to give the dog a broader area to explore or to shorten the length to keep the dog near you. Of course there are special leads for training purposes, and specially made leather harnesses, but these are not necessary for routine walks.

COLLAR

Your pup should get used to wearing a collar all the time since you will want to attach his ID tags to it. Plus, you have to attach the lead to something! A lightweight nylon collar is a good choice; make sure that it fits snugly enough so that the pup cannot wriggle out of it, but is loose enough so that it will not be

Select a strong nylon lead for your Cardigan from the wide selection available at most pet-supply outlets.

uncomfortably tight around the pup's neck. You should be able to fit a finger between the pup and the collar. It may take some time for your pup to get used to wearing the collar, but soon he will not even notice that it is there. Choke collars are made for training, but should only be used by an experienced handler.

FOOD AND WATER BOWLS

Your pup will need two bowls, one for food and one for water. You may want two sets of bowls, one for inside and one for outside, depending on where the dog will be fed and where he will be spending time. Stainless steel or sturdy plastic bowls are popular choices. Plastic bowls are more

CHOOSE AN APPROPRIATE COLLAR

The **BUCKLE COLLAR** is the standard collar used for everyday purposes. Be sure that you adjust the buckle on growing puppies. Check it every day. It can become too tight overnight! These collars can be made of leather or nylon. Attach your dog's identification tags to this collar.

The **CHOKE COLLAR** is the usual collar recommended for training. It is constructed of highly polished steel so that it slides easily through the stainless steel loop. The idea is that the dog controls the pressure around its neck and he will stop pulling if the collar becomes uncomfortable. Never leave a choke collar on your dog when not training.

The **HALTER** is for a trained dog that has to be restrained to prevent running away, chasing a cat and the like. Considered the most humane of all collars, it is frequently used on smaller dogs for which collars are not comfortable.

Purchase a 'pooper scooper' to make the clean-up job more convenient.

Your local pet shop will have a variety of water and food bowls from which you can make a selection. Bowls are made of pottery, flexible plastic, thermo-set plastic (hard) and various metals including stainless steel.

chewable. Dogs tend not to chew on the steel variety, which can be sterilised. It is important to buy sturdy bowls since anything is in danger of being chewed by puppy teeth and you do not want your dog to be constantly chewing apart his bowl (for his safety and for your purse!).

CLEANING SUPPLIES

Until a pup is house-trained, you will be doing a lot of cleaning. 'Accidents' will occur, which is acceptable in the beginning because the puppy does not know any better. All you can do is be prepared to clean up any accidents. Old rags, towels,

TEETHING TIP
Puppies like soft toys for chewing. Because they are teething, soft items like stuffed toys soothe their aching gums.

newspapers and a safe disinfectant are good to have on hand.

BEYOND THE BASICS
The items previously discussed are the bare necessities. You will find out what else you need as you go along—grooming supplies, flea/tick protection, baby gates to partition a room, etc. These things will vary depending on your situation but it is important that you have everything you need to feed and make your Cardigan Welsh Corgi comfortable in his first few days at home.

PUPPY-PROOFING YOUR HOME
Aside from making sure that your Cardigan will be comfortable in your home, you also have to make sure that your home is safe for your Cardigan. This means taking precautions that your pup will not get into anything he should not get into and that there is nothing

PLAY'S THE THING
Teaching the puppy to play with his toys in running and fetching games is an ideal way to help the puppy develop muscle, learn motor skills and bond with you, his owner and master.

He also needs to learn how to inhibit his bite reflex and never to use his teeth on people, forbidden objects and other animals in play. Whenever you play with your puppy, you make the rules. This becomes an important message to your puppy in teaching him that you are the pack leader and control everything he does in life. Once your dog accepts you as his leader, your relationship with him will be cemented for life.

Bringing a new dog into your life means becoming responsible for its whole life, including its safety in your home and garden.

within his reach that may harm him should he sniff it, chew it, inspect it, etc. This probably seems obvious since, while you are primarily concerned with your pup's safety, at the same time you do not want your belongings to be ruined. Breakables should be placed out of reach if your dog is to have full run of the house, keeping in mind the Cardi's ever-wagging fox-brush tail! If he is to be limited to certain places within

the house, keep any potentially dangerous items in the 'off-limits' areas. An electrical cord can pose a danger should the puppy decide to taste it—and who is going to convince a pup that it would not make a great chew toy? Cords should be fastened tightly against the wall. If your dog is going to spend time in a crate, make sure that there is nothing near his crate that he can reach if he sticks his curious little nose or paws

DENTAL HEALTH

A dental examination is in order when the dog is between six months and one year of age so any permanent teeth that have erupted incorrectly can be corrected. It is important to begin a brushing routine, preferably using a two-sided brushing technique, whereby both sides of the tooth are brushed at the same time. Durable nylon and safe edible chews should be a part of your puppy's arsenal for good health, good teeth and pleasant breath. The vast majority of dogs three to four years old and older has diseases of the gums from lack of dental attention. Using the various types of dental chews can be very effective in controlling dental plaque.

a pup let loose in the garden will want to run and explore, and he should be granted that freedom. Cardigans are not climbers and are seldom inclined to dig as a matter of escape unless neglected and separated from their loved ones for too long a time. They are not wanderers, either; the tendency to wander is often the inspiration for a dog to dig or climb his way out of an enclosure.

Nonetheless, do not let a fence give you a false sense of security; you would be surprised how crafty (and persistent) a dog can be in working out how to wriggle under a fence and squeeze his way through small holes. The remedy is to make the fence well embedded into the ground and high enough so that it really is impossible for your dog to get out. Be sure to repair or secure any gaps in the fence. Check the fence periodically to ensure that it is in good shape and make repairs as needed; a very determined pup may return to the same spot to 'work on it' until he is able to get through.

FIRST TRIP TO THE VET

You have selected your puppy, and your home and family are ready. Now all you have to do is collect your Cardigan from the breeder and the fun begins, right? Well...not so fast. Something else you need to prepare is your pup's first trip to the veterinary surgeon.

through the openings. Just as you would with a child, keep all household cleaners and chemicals where the pup cannot reach them.

It is also important to make sure that the outside of your home is safe. Of course your puppy should never be unsupervised, but

PUPPY-PROOFING

Thoroughly puppy-proof your house before bringing your puppy home. Never use cockroach or rodent poisons in any area accessible to the puppy. Avoid the use of toilet cleaners. Most dogs are born with 'toilet sonar' and will take a drink if the lid is left open. Also keep the rubbish secured and out of reach.

Perhaps the breeder can recommend someone in the area who specialises in Corgis, or maybe you know some other Cardi owners who can suggest a good vet. Either way, you should have an appointment arranged for your pup before you pick him up.

The pup's first visit will consist of an overall examination to make sure that the pup does not have any problems that are not apparent to you. The veterinary surgeon will also set up a schedule for the pup's vaccina-tions; the breeder will inform you of which ones the pup has already received and the vet can continue from there.

INTRODUCTION TO THE FAMILY

Everyone in the house will be excited about the puppy's coming home and will want to pet him and play with him, but it is best to make the introduction low-key so as not to overwhelm the puppy. He is apprehensive already. It is the first time he has been separated from his mother and the breeder, and the ride to your home is likely to be the first time

CHEMICAL TOXINS

Scour your garage for potential puppy dangers. Remove weed killers, pesticides and antifreeze materials. Antifreeze is highly toxic and even a few drops can kill an adult dog. The sweet taste attracts the animal, who will quickly consume it from the floor or curbside.

NATURAL TOXINS

Examine your grass and garden landscaping before bringing your puppy home. Many varieties of plants have leaves, stems or flowers that are toxic if ingested, and you can depend on a curious puppy to investigate them. Ask your vet for information on poisonous plants or research them at your library.

himself with exploring for a while. Gradually, each person should spend some time with the pup, one at a time, crouching down to get as close to the pup's level as possible and letting him sniff their hands and petting him gently. He definitely needs human attention and he needs to be touched—this is how to form an immediate bond. Just remember that the pup is experiencing a lot of things for the first time, at the same time. There are new people, new noises, new smells and new things to investigate: so be gentle, be affectionate and be as comforting as you can be.

PUP'S FIRST NIGHT HOME

You have travelled home with your new charge safely in his crate. He's been to the vet for a thorough check-up; he's been weighed, his papers examined; perhaps he's even been vaccinated and wormed as well. He's met the family, licked the whole family, including the excited children and the less-than-happy cat. He's explored his area, his new bed, the garden and anywhere else he's been permitted. He's eaten his first meal at home and relieved himself in the proper place. He's heard lots of new sounds, smelled new friends and seen more of the outside world than ever before.

That was just the first day! He's worn out and is ready for bed...or so you think!

STRESS-FREE

Some experts in canine health advise that stress during a dog's early years of development can compromise and weaken his immune system, and may trigger the potential for a shortened life expectancy. They emphasise the need for happy and stress-free growing-up years.

he has been in a car. The last thing you want to do is smother him, as this will only frighten him further. This is not to say that human contact is not extremely necessary at this stage, because this is the time when a connection between the pup and his human family is formed. Gentle petting and soothing words should help console him, as well as just putting him down and letting him explore on his own (under your watchful eye, of course).

The pup may approach the family members or may busy

THE RIDE HOME

Taking your dog from the breeder to your home in a car can be a very uncomfortable experience for both of you. The puppy will have been taken from his warm, friendly, safe environment and brought into a strange new environment—an environment that moves! Be prepared for loose bowels, urination, crying, whining and even fear biting. With proper love and encouragement when you arrive home, the stress of the trip should quickly disappear.

It's puppy's first night and you are ready to say 'Good night'—keep in mind that this is puppy's first night ever to be sleeping alone. His dam and littermates are no longer at paw's length and he's a bit scared, cold and lonely. Be reassuring to your new family member. This is not the time to spoil him and give in to his inevitable whining.

A FORTNIGHT'S GRACE

It will take at least two weeks for your puppy to become accustomed to his new surroundings. Give him lots of love, attention, handling, frequent opportunities to relieve himself, a diet he likes to eat and a place he can call his own.

Puppies whine. They whine to let others know where they are and hopefully to get company out of it. Place your pup in his new bed or crate in his room and close the door. Mercifully, he may fall asleep without a peep. When the inevitable occurs, ignore the whining: he is fine. Be strong and keep his interest in mind. Do not allow yourself to feel guilty and visit the pup. He will fall asleep eventually.

Many breeders recommend placing a piece of bedding from his former home in his new bed so that he recognises the scent of his littermates. Others still advise placing a hot water bottle in his bed for warmth. This latter may

Your Cardi's first night in your home will likely be his first time away from his mother. Be very sensitive to the needs of your puppy and he will adjust to his new home in no time.

MANNERS MATTER

During the socialisation process, a puppy should meet people, experience different environments and definitely be exposed to other canines. Through playing and interacting with other dogs, your puppy will learn lessons, ranging from controlling the pressure of his jaws by biting his littermates to the inner-workings of the canine pack that he will apply to his human relationships for the rest of his life. That is why removing a puppy from its litter too early (before eight weeks) can be detrimental to the pup's development.

be a good idea provided the pup doesn't attempt to suckle—he'll get good and wet and may not fall asleep so fast.

Puppy's first night can be somewhat stressful for the pup and his new family. Remember that you are setting the tone of nighttime at your house. Unless you want to play with your pup every evening at 10 p.m., midnight and 2 a.m., don't initiate the habit. Your family will thank you, and so will your pup!

PREVENTING PUPPY PROBLEMS

SOCIALISATION

Now that you have done all of the preparatory work and have helped your pup get accustomed to his new home and family, it is about time for you to have some fun! Socialising your Cardigan Welsh Corgi pup gives you the opportu-

HOW VACCINES WORK

If you've just bought a puppy, you surely know the importance of having your pup vaccinated, but do you understand how vaccines work? Vaccines contain the same bacteria or viruses that cause the disease you want to prevent, but they have been chemically modified so that they don't cause any harm. Instead, the vaccine causes your dog to produce antibodies that fight the harmful bacteria. Thus, if your pup is exposed to the disease in the future, the antibodies will destroy the viruses or bacteria.

PROPER SOCIALISATION

The socialisation period for puppies is from age 8 to 16 weeks. This is the time when puppies need to leave their birth family and take up residence with their new owners, where they will meet many new people, other pets, etc. Failure to be adequately socialised can cause the dog to grow up fearing others and being shy and unfriendly due to a lack of self-confidence.

nity to show off your new friend, and your pup gets to reap the benefits of being an adorable furry creature that people will want to pet and, in general, think is absolutely precious!

Besides getting to know his new family, your puppy should be exposed to other people, animals and situations, but of course he must not come into close contact with dogs you don't know well until his course of injections is fully complete. This will help him become well adjusted as he grows up and less prone to being timid or fearful of the new things he will encounter. Your pup's sociali-sation began with the breeder but now it is your responsibility to continue it. The socialisation he receives up until the age of 12 weeks is the most critical, as this is the time when he forms his

impressions of the outside world. Be especially careful during the eight-to-ten-week period, also known as the fear period. The interaction he receives during this time should be gentle and reassuring. Lack of socialisation can manifest itself in fear and aggression as the dog grows up. He needs lots of human contact, affection, handling and exposure to other animals. Cardis are not inherently quarrelsome, but they will not tolerate aggression on the part of other dogs. A Cardigan will not back down to a bully, no matter how large and imposing that bully might be.

Once your pup has received his necessary vaccinations, feel free to take him out and about (on his lead, of course). Walk him around the neighbourhood, take him on your daily errands, let people pet him, let him meet

MEET THE WORLD

Thorough socialisation includes not only meeting new people but also being introduced to new experiences such as riding in the car, having his coat brushed, hearing the television, walking in a crowd—the list is endless. The more your pup experiences, and the more positive the experiences are, the less of a shock and the less frightening it will be for your pup to encounter new things.

TRAINING TIP
Training your puppy takes much patience and can be frustrating at times, but you should see results from your efforts. If you have a puppy that seems untrainable, take him to a trainer or behaviourist. The dog may have a personality problem that requires the help of a professional, or perhaps you need help in learning how to train your dog.

unintentionally handle a pup too roughly, or an overzealous pup can playfully nip a little too hard. You want to make socialisation experiences positive ones. What a pup learns during this very formative stage will affect his attitude toward future encounters. You want your dog to be comfortable around everyone. A pup that has a bad experience with a child may grow up to be a dog that is shy around or aggressive toward children.

CONSISTENCY IN TRAINING
Dogs, being pack animals, naturally need a leader, or else they try to establish dominance in their packs. When you welcome a dog into your family, the choice of who becomes the leader and who

other dogs and pets, etc. Puppies do not have to try to make friends; there will be no shortage of people who will want to introduce themselves. Just make sure that you carefully supervise each meeting. If the neighbourhood children want to say hello, for example, that is great—children and pups most often make great companions. Sometimes an excited child can

FINANCIAL RESPONSIBILITY
Grooming tools, collars, leashes, dog beds and, of course, toys will be an expense to you when you first obtain your pup, and the cost will continue throughout your dog's lifetime. If your puppy damages or destroys your possessions (as most puppies surely will!) or something belonging to a neighbour, you can calculate additional expense. There is also flea and pest control, which every dog owner faces more than once. You must be able to handle the financial responsibility of owning a dog.

HOME WITH THE MANGE

Many young dogs suffer from demodectic mange, sometimes called red mange. While all breeds of dog have suffered from demodectic mange, short-coated breeds are at a greater risk. The mange manifests itself as localised infections on the face, muzzle, neck and limbs. The symptoms include hair loss and red, scaly skin. Vets routinely treat demodectic mange so that secondary infections are avoided. Many breeders remove known carriers from their programmes.

becomes the 'pack' is entirely up to you! Your pup's intuitive quest for dominance, coupled with the fact that it is nearly impossible to look at an adorable Cardigan pup with his lop-sided ears and not cave in, give the pup almost an unfair advantage in getting the upper hand! A pup will definitely test the waters to see what he can and cannot do. Do not give in to those pleading eyes—stand your ground when it comes to disciplining the pup and make sure that all family members do the same. It will only confuse the pup when Mother tells him to keep off the sofa when he is used to sitting up there with Father to watch the nightly news. Avoid discrepancies by having all

members of the household decide on the rules before the pup even comes home...and be consistent in enforcing them! Early training shapes the dog's personality, so you cannot be unclear in what you expect.

COMMON PUPPY PROBLEMS

The best way to prevent puppy problems is to be proactive in stopping an undesirable behaviour as soon as it starts. The old saying 'You can't teach an old dog new tricks' does not necessarily hold true, but it is true that it is much easier to discourage bad behaviour in a young developing pup than to wait until the pup's bad behaviour becomes the adult dog's bad habit.

NO CHOCOLATE!

Use treats to bribe your dog into a desired behaviour. Try small pieces of hard cheese or freeze-dried liver. Never offer chocolate, as it has toxic qualities for dogs.

There are some problems that are especially prevalent in puppies as they develop.

NIPPING

As puppies start to teethe, they feel the need to sink their teeth into anything available...unfortunately that includes your fingers, arms, hair and toes. You may find this behaviour cute for the first five seconds...until you feel just how sharp those puppy teeth are. This is something you want to discourage immediately and consistently with a firm 'No!' (or whatever number of firm 'Nos' it takes for him to understand that you mean business). Then replace your finger with an appropriate chew toy. While this behaviour is merely annoying when the dog is young, it can become dangerous as your Cardigan Welsh Corgi's adult teeth grow in and his jaws develop, and he continues to think it is okay to gnaw on human appendages. Your Cardigan Welsh Corgi does not mean any harm with a friendly nip, but he also does not know his own strength.

CRYING/WHINING

Your pup will often cry, whine, whimper, howl or make some type of commotion when he is left alone. This is basically his way of calling out for attention to make sure that you know he is there and that you have not forgotten about him. He feels insecure

CHEWING TIPS

Chewing goes hand in hand with nipping in the sense that a teething puppy is always looking for a way to soothe his aching gums. In this case, instead of chewing on you, he may have taken a liking to your favourite shoe or something else which he should not be chewing. Again, realise that this is a normal canine behaviour that does not need to be discouraged, only redirected. Your pup just needs to be taught what is acceptable to chew on and what is off limits. Consistently tell him NO when you catch him chewing on something forbidden and give him a chew toy. Conversely, praise him when you catch him chewing on something appropriate. In this way you are discouraging the inappropriate behaviour and reinforcing the desired behaviour. The puppy chewing should stop after his adult teeth have come in, but an adult dog continues to chew for various reasons—perhaps because he is bored, perhaps to relieve tension or perhaps he just likes to chew. That is why it is important to redirect his chewing when he is still young.

when he is left alone, when you are out of the house and he is in his crate or when you are in another part of the house and he cannot see you. The noise he is making is an expression of the anxiety he feels at being alone, so

PUPPY PROBLEMS

The majority of problems that are commonly seen in young pups will disappear as your dog gets older. However, how you deal with problems when he is young will determine how he reacts to discipline as an adult dog. It is important to establish who is boss (hopefully it will be you!) right away when you are first bonding with your dog. This bond will set the tone for the rest of your life together.

he needs to be taught that being alone is okay. You are not actually training the dog to stop making noise, you are training him to feel comfortable when he is alone and thus removing the need for him to make the noise. This is where the crate with cosy bedding and a toy comes in handy. You want to know that he is safe when you are

MENTAL AND DENTAL

Toys not only help your puppy get the physical and mental stimulation he needs but also provide a great way to keep his teeth clean. Hard rubber or nylon toys, especially those constructed with grooves, are designed to scrape away plaque, preventing bad breath and gum infection.

not there to supervise, and you know that he will be safe in his crate rather than roaming freely about the house. In order for the pup to stay in his crate without making a fuss, he needs to be comfortable in his crate. On that note, it is extremely important that the crate is never used as a form of punishment, or the pup will have a negative association with the crate.

Some low-to-the-ground fun for Rachel Stoltzman, age six, with Libbie, age one year.

Accustom the pup to the crate in short, gradually increasing time intervals in which you put him in the crate, maybe with a treat, and stay in the room with him. If he cries or makes a fuss, do not go to him, but stay in his sight. Gradually he will realise that staying in his crate is all right without your help, and it will not be so traumatic for him when you are not around. You may want to leave the radio on softly when you leave the house; the sound of human voices may be comforting to him.

FEEDING YOUR CARDIGAN

There is no simple way to answer the question of 'What is the best food to give your Cardigan?' We have spoken to successful Corgi breeders in many parts of the world and each breeder seems to have his or her own tried-and-true method. Probably the best answer to the question is to feed what works best in light of the dog's weight and general condition. This may not always be what the dog likes best! Who can tell you just what food that is? We sincerely recommend you consult with the breeder from whom you purchased your Cardigan and your veterinary surgeon.

The correct amount of food to maintain a Cardigan Corgi's optimal condition varies as much from dog to dog as it does from human to human. It is impossible to state any specific amount of food your dog should be given. Much depends upon how much your dog exercises. A Cardi that spends the entire day working livestock will need considerably more food than the house dog whose exercise is limited to 15 or 20 minutes a day retrieving a ball.

Generally speaking, the amount of food for a normally active Cardigan is the amount that the dog will eat readily within about 15 minutes of being given the meal. What your dog does not eat in that amount of time should be taken up and discarded. Leaving food out for extended periods of time can lead to erratic and finicky eating habits.

The Cardigan was originally bred to be a working dog. Meals

FEEDING TIP

You must store your dried dog food carefully. Open packages of dog food quickly lose their vitamin value, usually within 90 days of being opened. Mould spores and vermin could also contaminate the food.

were sporadic, of questionable nutritious value and came only after a long gruelling day's work. Today's Cardigan has an appetite every bit as big as its ancestors, but he usually has far less work to do. Cardis can gain weight very easily if their food intake is not controlled and they are not given an opportunity to get sufficient exercise.

Excess weight puts great stress on a Cardi's back and legs, and can lead to serious and irreversible problems. A good rule of thumb to follow in determining whether or not a Corgi is receiving the proper amount of food is to closely monitor the dog's condition. You should be able to feel the ribs and backbone through a slight layer of muscle and fat.

Fresh water and a properly prepared balanced diet, containing the essential nutrients in correct proportions, are all that a healthy dog needs to be offered. If your Cardigan will not eat the food offered, it is because he is

FOOD PREFERENCE

Selecting the best dried dog food is difficult. There is no majority consensus among veterinary scientists as to the value of nutrient analyses (protein, fat, fibre, moisture, ash, cholesterol, minerals, etc.). All agree that feeding trials are what matter, but you also have to consider the individual dog. The dog's weight, age and activity level, and what pleases his taste, all must be considered. It is probably best to take the advice of your veterinary surgeon. Every dog's dietary require-ments vary, even during the lifetime of a particular dog.

If your dog is fed a good dried food, it does not require supple-ments of meat or vegetables. Dogs do appreciate a little variety in their diets, so you may choose to stay with the same brand but vary the flavour. Alternatively, you may wish to add a little flavoured stock to give a difference to the taste.

TEST FOR PROPER DIET

A good test for proper diet is the colour, odour and firmness of your dog's stool. A healthy dog usually produces three semi-hard stools per day. The stools should have no unpleasant odour. They should be the same colour from excretion to excretion.

CHANGE IN DIET

As your dog's caretaker, you know the importance of keeping his diet consistent, but sometimes when you run out of food or if you're on holiday, you have to make a change quickly. Some dogs will experience digestive problems, but most will not. If you are planning on changing your dog's menu, do so gradually to ensure that your dog will not have any problems. Over a period of four to five days, slowly add some new food to your dog's old food, increasing the percentage of new food each day.

either not hungry or ill. If the former is the case, the dog will eat when he is hungry. If you suspect the latter, an appointment with your veterinary surgeon is in order.

Dogs, whether Corgis or Great Danes, are carnivorous (meat-eating) animals, and while the vegetable content of your dog's diet should not be overlooked, a dog's physiology and anatomy are based upon carnivorous food acquisition. Protein and fat are absolutely essential in a dog's diet. The animal protein and fat your dog needs can be replaced by some vegetable proteins, but the amounts and types require a better understanding of nutrition than most people have.

A great deal of research is conducted by manufacturers of the leading brands of dog food to determine the ideal balance of minerals, protein, carbohydrates and trace elements required for a

TIPPING THE SCALES

Good nutrition is vital to your dog's health, but many people end up over-feeding or giving unnecessary supplements. Here are some common doggie diet don'ts:
• Adding milk, yoghurt and cheese to your dog's diet may seem like a good idea for coat and skin care, but dairy products are very fattening and can cause indigestion.
• Diets high in fat will not cause heart attacks in dogs but will certainly cause your dog to gain weight.
• Most importantly, don't assume your dog will simply stop eating once he doesn't need any more food. Given the chance, he will eat you out of house and home!

THE CANINE GOURMET

Your dog does not prefer a fresh bone. Indeed, he wants it properly aged and, if given such a treat indoors, he is more likely to try to bury it in the carpet than he is to settle in for a good chew! If you have a garden, give him such delicacies outside and guide him to a place suitable for his 'bone yard.' He will carefully place the treasure in its earthy vault and seemingly forget about it. Trust me, his seeming distaste or lack of thanks for your thoughtfulness is not that at all. He will return in a few days to inspect the bone, perhaps to re-bury it, and when it is just right, he will relish it as much as you do that cooked-to-perfection steak. If he is in a concrete or bricked kennel run, he will be especially frustrated at the hopelessness of the situation. He will vacillate between ignoring it completely, giving it a few licks to speed the curing process with saliva and trying to hide it behind the water bowl! When the bone has aged a bit, he will set to work on it.

by weight. The major ingredient is listed first, the next most prominent follows and so on down the line. Whether tinned or dried, look for a food in which the main ingredient is derived from meat, poultry or fish. Remember, you can not purchase a top-quality dog food for the same price as one that lacks the nutritional value you are looking for. In many cases you will find not only that your Cardigan

DO DOGS HAVE TASTE BUDS?

Watching a dog 'wolf' or gobble his food, seemingly without chewing, leads an owner to wonder whether their dogs can taste anything. Yes, dogs have taste buds, with sensory perception of sweet, salty and sour. Puppies are born with fully mature taste buds.

dog's well-being. Dog food manufacturing has become so sophisticated that it is now possible to buy food for dogs with almost any kind of lifestyle, from sedentary to highly active.

Dog food must list all of its ingredients in descending order

needs less of the better food but also that there will be less faecal waste.

The highly fortified commercial dog foods seldom require additional vitamin supplementation. In special instances, such as during critical puppy growth periods or during the bitch's pregnancy or lactation, your vet may recommend supplementation. Even at that, only professionally recommended dosages must be given.

'DOES THIS COLLAR MAKE ME LOOK FAT?'

While humans may obsess about how they look and how trim their bodies are, many people believe that extra weight on their dogs is a good thing. The truth is, pets should not be over- or under-weight, as both can lead to or signal sickness. In order to tell how fit your pet is, run your hands over his ribs. Are his ribs buried under a layer of fat or are they sticking out considerably? If your pet is within his normal weight range, you should be able to feel the ribs easily, but they should not protrude abnormally. If you stand above him, the outline of his body should resemble an hourglass. Some breeds do tend to be leaner while some are a bit stockier, but making sure your dog is the right weight for his breed will certainly contribute to his good health.

FEEDING TIPS

Dog food must be at room temperature, neither too hot nor too cold. Fresh water, changed daily and served in a clean bowl, is mandatory, especially when feeding dried food.

Never feed your dog from the table while you are eating, and never feed your dog leftovers from your own meal. They usually contain too much fat and too much seasoning.

Dogs must chew their food. Hard pellets are excellent; soups and slurries are to be avoided.

Don't add leftovers or any extras to normal dog food. The normal food is usually balanced, and adding something extra destroys the balance.

Except for age-related changes, dogs do not require dietary variations. They can be fed the same diet, day after day, without becoming ill.

When selecting your dog's diet, three stages of development must be considered: the puppy stage, adult stage and the veteran stage.

PUPPY STAGE

Puppies instinctively want to suck milk from their mother's teats and a normal puppy will exhibit this behaviour from just a few moments following birth. If puppies do not attempt to suckle within the first half-hour or so, they should be encouraged to do so by placing them on the nipples, having selected ones with plenty of milk. This early milk supply is important in providing colostrum to protect the puppies during the first eight to ten weeks of their lives. Although a mother's milk is much better than any milk formula, despite there being some excellent ones available, if the puppies do not feed, you will have to feed them yourself. For those with less experience, advice from a veterinary surgeon is important so that you feed not only the right quantity of milk but that of correct quality, fed at suitably frequent intervals, usually every two hours during the first few days of life.

Puppies should be allowed to nurse from their mothers for about the first six weeks, although from the third or fourth week the breeder should begin to introduce small portions of suitable solid food. Most breeders like to introduce alternate milk and meat meals initially, building up to weaning time.

By the time the puppies are seven or a maximum of eight weeks old, they should be fully weaned and fed solely on a proprietary puppy food. Selection of the most suitable, good-quality diet at this time is essential, for a puppy's fastest growth rate is during the first year of life. Veterinary surgeons are usually able to offer advice in this regard and, although the frequency of meals will have been reduced over time, only when a young dog has reached the age of about eight to ten months should an adult diet be fed.

Puppy and junior diets should be well balanced for the needs of your dog, so that except in certain circumstances additional

Competition during feeding time entices the puppies' appetites. The struggle for the best nipple is replaced by the quest for a secure place at the feeding bowl.

vitamins, minerals and proteins will not be required.

ADULT DIETS

A dog is considered an adult when it has stopped growing, so in general the diet of a Cardigan can be changed to an adult one at about eight to ten months of age. This means it can be given one main meal a day, preferably at the same time each evening. Some owners prefer to divide the single meal into two smaller meals, given morning and evening.

Meals can be supplemented by a morning or mid-day snack, and for this we highly recommend hard dog biscuits made for large dogs. Remember, the only small things about a Cardigan Corgi are his legs. A Cardi has powerful jaws and can handle those hard biscuits with ease. These not only prove to be a much anticipated treat, but do wonders toward maintaining healthy gums and teeth.

As far as what you feed, again you should rely upon your veterinary surgeon or dietary specialist to recommend an acceptable

> **GRAIN-BASED DIETS**
> Some less expensive dog foods are based on grains and other plant proteins. While these products may appear to be attractively priced, many breeders prefer a diet based on animal proteins and believe that they are more conducive to your dog's health. Many grain-based diets rely on soy protein, which may cause flatulence (passing gas).
>
> There are many cases, however, when your dog might require a special diet. These special requirements should only be recommended by your veterinary surgeon.

maintenance diet. Major dog food manufacturers specialise in this type of food, and it is merely necessary for you to select the one best suited to your dog's needs. Active dogs have different requirements than sedate dogs and may require less food, lest they gain weight. Depending upon individual dog and general condition (weight, activity, etc.), a Cardigan should be able to stay on a maintenance diet until about six or seven years old.

VETERAN DIETS

As dogs get older, their metabolism changes. The older dog usually exercises less, moves more slowly and sleeps more. This change in lifestyle and

Puppies begin eating solid foods while at the breeder's kennel. Most pups are weaned by the age of six or seven weeks. It is advised to follow the advice of the breeder when selecting a brand of food for your Cardi pup.

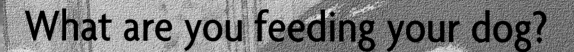

What are you feeding your dog?

Read the label on your dog food. Many dog foods only advise what 50—55% of the contents are, leaving the other 45% in doubt.

Calcium 1.3%
Fatty Acids 1.6%
Crude Fibre 4.6%
Moisture 11%
Crude Fat 14%
Crude Protein 22%
45.5% ? ? ?

DRINK, DRANK, DRUNK— MAKE IT A DOUBLE

In both humans and dogs, as well as most living organisms, water forms the major part of nearly every body tissue. Naturally, we take water for granted, but without it, life as we know it would cease.

For dogs, water is needed to keep their bodies functioning biochemi- cally. Additionally, water is needed to replace the water lost while panting. Unlike humans, who are able to sweat to dissipate heat, dogs must pant to cool down, thereby losing the vital water from their bodies needed to regulate their body temperatures. Humans lose electrolyte-containing products and other body-fluid components through sweating; dogs do not lose anything except water.

Water is essential always, but especially so when the weather is hot or humid or when your dog is exercising or working vigorously.

physiological performance requires a change in diet. Since these changes take place slowly, they might not be readily recognisable. What is easily recognisable is weight gain, a common concern for adult Corgis as well. By continuing to feed your dog the same adult-mainte- nance diet when it is slowing down metabolically, your dog will gain weight. Obesity in an older dog compounds the health problems that already accompany old age.

The geriatric or overweight Cardi needs a much lower-calorie diet than the growing puppy or adult dog of normal weight. It is also important to make sure your older dog gets its fair share of exercise each day. The old-timer may prefer to spend more of his day on the sofa than when he was a youngster, but moderate exercise even for the very old dog will keep your friend alive longer.

As your dog gets older, few of his organs function up to par. The kidneys slow down and the intestines become less efficient. These age-related factors are best handled with a change in diet and a change in feeding schedule to give smaller portions that are more easily digested.

There is no single best diet for every older dog. While many dogs do well on light or senior diets, other dogs do better on puppy diets or other special premium diets such as lamb and rice. Be sensitive to your senior Cardigan's diet and this will help control other problems that may arise with your old friend.

WATER

Just as your dog needs proper nutrition from his food, water is an essential 'nutrient' as well. Water keeps the dog's body properly hydrated and promotes normal function of the body's systems. During house-training it is necessary to keep an eye on how much water your Cardigan is drinking, but once he is reliably trained he should have access to clean fresh water at all times, especially if you feed dried food. Make certain that the dog's water bowl is clean, and change the water often.

EXERCISE

The Cardigan was bred to work a full day, and that ability and need

EXERCISE ALERT!

You should be careful where you exercise your dog. Many country-side areas have been sprayed with chemicals that are highly toxic to both dogs and humans. Never allow your dog to eat grass or drink from puddles on either public or private grounds, as the run-off water may contain chemicals from sprays and herbicides.

remain with the breed to this day. A well-exercised Cardi can live happily in a flat in a big city if, and only if, he is in fact sufficiently exercised. The bored, inactive Cardigan would be extremely unhappy and more than capable of wreaking havoc in a confining environment.

Taking into consideration the Cardi's short legs, he is capable of and delighted at being a jogging companion. It is important, however, to use good judgement in any exercise programme. Begin slowly and increase the distance to be covered very gradually over an extended period of time. Use special precautions in hot weather. High temperatures and forced exercise are a dangerous combination.

Needless to say, puppies should never be forced to exercise. Normally, they are little dynamos of energy and keep

Puppies will get enough exercise from their regular play in the garden. Do not subject the growing pup to vigorous exercise as this may aggravate possible joint and back problems.

The best exercise for any dog is the companionship of another dog. This Cardigan is enjoying a game of fetch (and keep-away) with his Swedish cousin, the Vallhund.

Some Cardigans need a little encouragement in the exercise department. Don't let your Corgi become a lazy 'couch potato.' Bandit is nine years of age, and sharing with his one-year-old playmate, Bebe, the joys of napping.

themselves busy all day long, with bursts of activity interspersed with frequent naps. A Corgi should never be subjected to an extended jogging programme before it is 18 months of age and fully mature. Because of its long back and short-legged conformation, the Cardigan can be susceptible to back and joint problems during the developmental months. The Cardigan puppy must be kept from going down stairs or jumping off furniture until it is at least seven or eight months of age. During these developmental months, the Cardigan's forequarter assembly is in somewhat of a fragile state and such activities, along with too much or too strenuous exercise, can cause serious injury.

The best exercise for a Cardi is that acquired in the pursuit of the many organised activities for which the breed is particularly well suited. Herding trials, agility, flyball and obedience activities exercise both the Cardigan's mind and body. There is no better way to ensure your Cardigan Corgi of a happy, healthy existence.

GROOMING

BRUSHING

Your Corgi will not require much time or equipment in the way of grooming, but that is not to say that he needs no coat care at all in this respect. Regular brushing keeps the coat clean, odour-free and healthy. Corgis will cast their coats twice a year. Brushing is an absolute necessity at these times, particularly if your dog spends time indoors.

Regular grooming also gives you the opportunity to keep on top of your dog's home health care needs. Such things as clipping nails, cleaning ears and checking teeth can be taken care of during the time set aside for grooming.

Investing in a grooming table that has a non-slip top and an 'arm' with a 'noose' can make all of these activities infinitely easier. These tables are available at pet shops and it is important to choose a table of a height that

GROOMING EQUIPMENT

How much grooming equipment you purchase will depend on how much grooming you are going to do. Here are some basics:

- Natural bristle brush
- Rubber brush
- Metal comb
- Hound glove
- Blaster
- Rubber mat
- Dog shampoo
- Spray hose attachment
- Ear cleaner
- Cotton wipes
- Towels
- Nail clippers

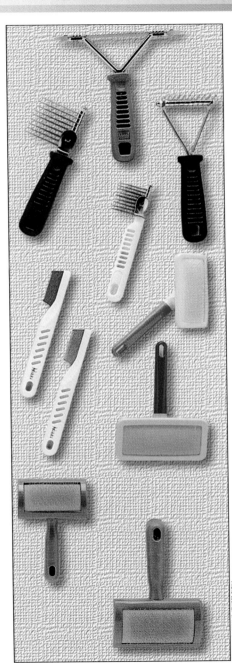

Your local pet shop will have a variety of grooming tools with which you can successfully groom your Cardi. Fortunately, Cardis do not require a great deal of grooming.

PHOTO COURTESY OF MIKKI PET PRODUCTS.

Acclimate the puppy to the grooming routine from a young age. Although Cardigans do not require extensive grooming, it pays to have a cooperative dog when it comes to brushing.

This adult Cardi is enjoying his grooming time with his owner. If you purchase a good quality brush, it can be used both for the puppy and adult Cardi.

allows you to stand or sit comfortably while you are working on your dog. A grooming table that has an arm and a noose (which looks and functions like a lead) keeps the dog from fidgeting about or deciding that he has had enough grooming.

Invest in a good stiff bristle brush, a steel comb and nail clippers or a drummel, which

grinds the nails down rather than actually cutting them. You will be using this equipment for many years, so buy the best equipment you can afford.

The Cardigan is a natural breed with a coat that requires no clipping or trimming. Proper brushing and a few snips of the scissors around the feet are all the grooming it will ever need. Brush your Cardi with the lie of the hair and use the steel comb on the longer hair of the 'pants' on the dog's rear legs and on the tail. At moulting time, there will be a tremendous amount of hair collected in your brush and comb. You can hasten this process by giving your Cardi a warm bath once the shedding has begun. This loosens the hair and, though you may think your dog will end up completely bald after moulting, fear not—once the dead coat has been removed, the shedding stops and new hair growth will begin.

BATHING

Dogs do not need to be bathed as often as humans, but regular bathing is essential for healthy skin and a healthy, shiny coat. Again, like most anything, if you accustom your pup to being bathed as a puppy, it will be second nature by the time he grows up. You want your dog to be at ease in the bath or else it could end up a wet, soapy, messy

the coat. Check the water temperature to make sure that it is neither too hot nor too cold.

Next, apply shampoo to the dog's coat and work it into a good

SOAP IT UP

The use of human soap products like shampoo, bubble bath and hand soap can be damaging to a dog's coat and skin. Human products are too strong; they remove the protective oils coating the dog's hair and skin that make him water-resistant. Use only shampoo made especially for dogs. You may like to use a medicated shampoo, which will help to keep external parasites at bay.

BATHING BEAUTY

Once you are sure that the dog is thoroughly rinsed, squeeze the excess water out of his coat with your hand and dry him with a heavy towel. You may choose to use a blaster on his coat or just let it dry naturally. In cold weather, never allow your dog outside with a wet coat.

There are 'dry bath' products on the market, which are sprays and powders intended for spot cleaning, that can be used between regular baths if necessary. They are not substitutes for regular baths, but they are easy to use for touch-ups as they do not require rinsing.

ordeal for both of you!

Brush your Cardigan thoroughly before wetting his coat. This will get rid of most mats and tangles, which are harder to remove when the coat is wet. Make certain that your dog has a good non-slip surface to stand on. Begin by wetting the dog's coat. A shower or hose attachment is necessary for thoroughly wetting and rinsing

Nail Maintenance

Nail Casing

Quick

Cut Line

Dark-Coloured Nails

With black or dark nails, it's best to clip only the tip of the nail or to use a file.

Light-Coloured Nails

In light-coloured nails, clipping is much simpler because you can see the vein (or quick) that grows inside the casing.

lather. You should purchase a shampoo that is made for dogs. Do not use a product made for human hair. Wash the head last; you do not want shampoo to drip into the dog's eyes while you are washing the rest of his body. Work the shampoo all the way down to the skin. You can use this opportunity to check the skin for any bumps, bites or other abnormalities. Do not neglect any area of the body—get all of the hard-to-reach places.

Once the dog has been thoroughly shampooed, he requires an equally thorough rinsing. Shampoo left in the coat can be irritating to the skin. Protect his eyes from the shampoo by shielding them with your hand and directing the flow of water in the opposite direction. You should also avoid getting water in the ear canal. Be prepared for your dog to shake out his coat—you might want to stand back, but make sure you have a hold on the dog to keep him from running through the house.

NAIL FILING

You can purchase an electric tool to grind down a dog's nails rather than cut them. Some dogs don't seem to mind the electric grinder but will object strongly to nail clippers. Talking it over with your veterinary surgeon will help you make the right choice.

EAR CLEANING

The ears should be kept clean with a cotton wipe and ear powder made especially for dogs. Be on the lookout for any signs of infection or ear mite infestation. If your Cardigan has been shaking his head or scratching at his ears frequently, this usually indicates a problem. If his ears have an unusual odour, this is a sure sign of mite infestation or infection, and a signal to have his ears checked by the veterinary surgeon.

NAILS AND FEET

During the grooming session is a good time to accustom your Cardigan to having its nails trimmed and having its feet inspected. Check between the toes for splinters and thorns, paying particular attention to any swollen or tender areas. In some areas there exists a weed called the fox-tail that has a barbed 'hook' in which the seed is carried. This hook easily finds its way into a dog's foot or between its toes and very quickly works its way deep into the dog's flesh, causing soreness and infection. These barbs are best removed by your vet before serious problems result.

Get in the routine of attending to your dog's nails every other week. If your Cardi is getting plenty of exercise on cement or rough hard pavement, the nails may stay sufficiently worn down.

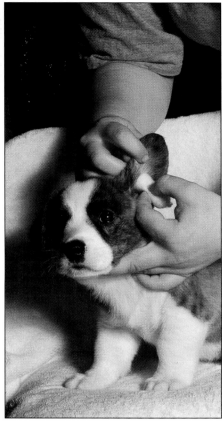

Your Cardigan's ears must be cleaned and inspected on a regular basis. Never probe into the dog's ears with a cotton bud, but instead use a piece of cotton or cotton wipe to clean any debris that is visible.

However, the nails of a Corgi that spends most of its time indoors or on grass when outdoors can grow long very quickly. Do not allow the nails to become overgrown and then expect to cut them back easily. They must then be trimmed with canine nail clippers, an electric nail grinder or a coarse file made expressly for that purpose. Regardless of which nail-trimming device is used, you must proceed with caution and

the 'quick.' The quick grows close to the end of the nail and contains very sensitive nerve endings. If the nail is allowed to grow too long, it will be impossible to cut it back to a proper length without cutting into the quick. This causes severe pain to the dog and can also result in a great deal of bleeding that can be very difficult to stop.

Before you start cutting, make sure you can identify the quick in each nail. Keep some type of clotting agent on hand, such as a styptic pencil or styptic powder (the type used for shaving). This will stop the bleeding quickly when applied to the end of the cut nail, and can also be of use if the dog ever breaks a nail in some way. Do not panic if you cut the quick, just stop the bleeding and talk soothingly to your dog. Once he has calmed down, move on to the next nail, remembering to clip only a little at a time. This is particularly important with black-nailed dogs, where the quick is more difficult to see.

Hold your pup steady as you begin trimming his nails; you do not want him to make any sudden movements or run away. Talk to him soothingly and stroke him as you clip. Holding his foot in your hand, simply take off the end of each nail in one quick clip. You should find that you both become accustomed to the procedure rather quickly.

PEDICURE TIP

A dog that spends a lot of time outside on a hard surface, such as cement or pavement, will have his nails naturally worn down and may not need to have them trimmed as often, except maybe in the colder months when he is not outside as much. Regardless, it is best to get your dog accustomed to the nail-trimming procedure at an early age so that he is used to it. Some dogs are especially sensitive about having their feet touched, but if a dog has experienced it since puppyhood, it should not bother him.

remove only a small portion of the nail at a time.

Each nail has a blood vessel running through the centre called

TRAVEL TIP
The most extensive travel you do with your dog may be limited to trips to the veterinary surgeon's office—or you may decide to bring him along for long distances when the family goes on holiday. Whichever the case, it is important to consider your dog's safety while travelling.

TRAVELLING WITH YOUR DOG

Car Travel

You should accustom your Cardigan to riding in a car at an early age. You may or may not take him in the car often, but at the very least he will need to go to the vet and you do not want these trips to be traumatic for the dog or troublesome for you. The safest way for a dog to ride in the car is in his crate. If he uses a crate in the house, you can use the same crate for travel.

Put the pup in the crate and see how he reacts. If he seems uneasy, you can have a passenger hold him on his lap while you drive. Another option is a specially made safety harness for dogs, which straps the dog in much like a seat belt. Do not let the dog roam loose in the vehicle—this is very dangerous! If you should stop short, your dog can be thrown and injured. If the dog starts climbing on you and pestering you while you are driving, you will not be able to concentrate on the road. It is an unsafe situation for everyone— human and canine.

For long trips, be prepared to stop to let the dog relieve himself. Take with you whatever you need to clean up after him, including some paper kitchen towels and perhaps some old towelling for use should he have an accident in the car or suffer from travel sickness.

TRAVEL TIP
When travelling, never let your dog off-lead in a strange area. Your dog could run away out of fear, decide to chase a passing squirrel or cat or simply want to stretch his legs without restriction—if any of these happen, you might never see your canine friend again.

Should you decide not to take your Cardi on holiday with you, select a boarding facility that is well kept and run by responsible dog people.

Proper identification tags are a simple way to ensure that you will be able to retrieve your Cardi should he wander away from home.

Animals travel in a different area of the plane than human passengers so every rule must be strictly followed to prevent the risk of getting separated from your dog.

BOARDING

So you want to take a family holiday—and you want to include all members of the family. You would probably make arrangements for accommodation ahead of time anyway, but this is especially important when travelling with a dog. You do not want to make an overnight stop at the only place around for miles and find out that they do not allow dogs. Also, you do not want to reserve a place for your family without confirming that you are travelling with a dog because if it is against their policy you may not have a place to stay.

Alternatively, if you are travelling and choose not to bring your Cardigan, you will have to make arrangements for him while you are away. Some options are to take

AIR TRAVEL

While it is possible to take a dog on a flight within Britain, this is fairly unusual and advance permission is always required. The dog will be required to travel in a fibreglass crate and you should always check in advance with the airline regarding specific requirements. To help the dog be at ease, put one of his favourite toys in the crate with him. Do not feed the dog for at least six hours before the trip to minimise his need to relieve himself. However, certain regulations specify that water must always be made available to the dog in the crate.

Make sure your dog is properly identified and that your contact information appears on his ID tags and on his crate.

him to a neighbour's house to stay while you are gone, to have a trusted neighbour pop in often or stay at your house, or to bring your dog to a reputable boarding kennel. If you choose to board him at a kennel, you should visit in advance to see the facilities provided, how clean they are and where the dogs are kept. Talk to some of the employees and see how they treat the dogs—do they spend time with the dogs, play with them, exercise them, etc.? Also find out the kennel's policy on vaccinations and what they require. This is for all of the dogs' safety, since when dogs are kept together, there is a greater risk of diseases being passed from dog to dog.

IDENTIFICATION

Your Cardigan is your valued companion and friend. That is why you always keep a close eye on him and you have made sure that he cannot escape from the garden or wriggle out of his collar and run away from you. However, accidents can happen and there may come a time when your dog unexpectedly gets separated from you. If this unfortunate event should occur, the first thing on your mind will be finding him. Proper identification, including an ID tag, a tattoo and possibly a microchip, will increase the chances of his being returned to you safely and quickly.

IDENTIFICATION OPTIONS

As puppies become more and more expensive, especially those puppies of high quality for showing and/or breeding, they have a greater chance of being stolen. The usual collar dog tag is, of course, easily removed. But there are two more permanent techniques that have become widely used for identification.

The puppy microchip implantation involves the injection of a small microchip, about the size of a corn kernel, under the skin of the dog. If your dog shows up at a clinic or shelter, or is offered for resale under less than savoury circumstances, it can be positively identified by the microchip. The microchip is scanned, and a registry quickly identifies you as the owner. This is not only protection against theft, but should the dog run away or go chasing a squirrel and become lost, you have a fair chance of his being returned to you.

Tattooing is done on various parts of the dog, from his belly to his cheeks. The number tattooed can be your telephone number or any other number that you can easily memorise. When professional dog thieves see a tattooed dog, they usually lose interest. Both microchipping and tattooing can be done at your local veterinary clinic. For the safety of our dogs, no laboratory facility or dog broker will accept a tattooed dog as stock.

Living with an untrained dog is a lot like owning a piano that you do not know how to play—it is a nice object to look at but it does not do much more than that to bring you pleasure. Now try taking piano lessons and suddenly the piano comes alive and brings forth magical sounds and rhythms that set your heart singing and your body swaying.

The same is true with your Cardigan Welsh Corgi. Any dog is a big responsibility and if not trained sensibly may develop unacceptable behaviour that annoys you or could even cause family friction.

To train your Cardigan, you may like to enrol in an obedience class. Teach him good manners as you learn how and why he behaves the way he does. Find out how to communicate with your dog and how to recognise and understand his communications with you. Suddenly the dog takes on a new role in your life—he is clever, interesting, well-behaved and fun to be with. He demonstrates his bond of devotion to you daily. In other words, your Cardigan does wonders for your ego because he constantly reminds you that you are not only his leader, you are his hero!

Those involved with teaching dog obedience and counselling owners about their dogs' behaviour have discovered some interesting facts about dog ownership. For example, training dogs when they are puppies results in the highest rate of success in developing well-mannered and well-adjusted adult dogs. Training an older dog, from six months to six years of age, can produce almost equal results providing that the owner accepts the dog's slower rate of learning capability and is willing to work patiently to help the dog succeed at developing to his fullest potential. Unfortunately, many owners of untrained adult dogs lack the patience factor, so they do not persist until their dogs are successful at learning particular behaviours.

Training a puppy aged 10 to 16 weeks (20 weeks at the most) is like working with a dry sponge in a pool of water. The pup soaks up whatever you show him and constantly looks for more things to do and learn. At this early age, his body is not yet producing hormones, and therein lies the reason for such a high rate of success. Without hormones, he is focused on his owners and not particularly interested in investigating other places, dogs, people, etc. You are his leader: his provider of food, water, shelter and security. He latches onto you and wants to stay close. He will usually follow you from room to room, will not let you out of his sight when you are outdoors with him and will respond in like manner to the people and animals you encounter. If you greet a friend warmly, he will be happy to greet the person as well. If, however, you are hesitant, even anxious, about the approach of a stranger, he will respond accordingly.

Once the puppy begins to produce hormones, his natural curiosity emerges and he begins to investigate the world around him. It is at this time when you may notice that the untrained dog begins to wander away from you and even ignore your commands to stay close. When this behaviour becomes a problem, the owner has two choices: get rid of the dog or train him. It is strongly urged that you choose the latter option.

There are usually classes within a reasonable distance from the owner's home, but you can also do a lot to train your dog yourself. Sometimes there are

Cardigans have great capacities for training. This Cardigan has been trained to compete in agility trials.

classes available but the tuition is too costly. Whatever the circumstances, the solution to the problem of lack of lesson availability lies within the pages of this book.

This chapter is devoted to helping you train your Cardigan Welsh Corgi at home. If the recommended procedures are followed faithfully, you may expect positive results that will

HONOUR AND OBEY

Dogs are the most honourable animals in existence. They consider another species (humans) as their own. They interface with you. You are their leader. Corgis perceive children to be on their level; their actions around small children are different from their behaviour around their adult masters.

REAP THE REWARDS

If you start with a normal, healthy dog and give him time, patience and some carefully executed lessons, you will reap the rewards of that training for the life of the dog. And what a life it will be! The two of you will find immeasurable pleasure in the companionship you have built together with love, respect and understanding.

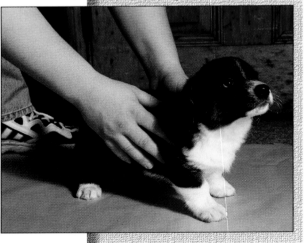

prove rewarding both to you and your dog.

Whether your new charge is a puppy or a mature adult, the methods of teaching and the techniques we use in training basic behaviours are the same. After all, no dog, whether puppy or adult, likes harsh or inhumane methods. All creatures, however, respond favourably to gentle motivational methods and sincere praise and encouragement. Now let us get started.

HOUSE-TRAINING

You can train a puppy to relieve itself wherever you choose, but this must be somewhere suitable. You should bear in mind from the outset that when your puppy is old enough to go out in public places, any canine deposits must be removed at once. You will always have to carry with you a small plastic bag or 'poop-scoop.'

Outdoor training includes

THE HAND THAT FEEDS
To a dog's way of thinking, your hands are like his mouth in terms of a defence mechanism. If you squeeze him too tightly, he might just bite you because that would be his normal response. This is not aggressive biting and, although all biting should be discouraged, you need the discipline in learning how to handle your dog.

such surfaces as grass, soil and cement. Indoor training usually means training your dog to newspaper.

When deciding on the surface and location that you will want your Cardigan to use, be sure it is going to be permanent. Training your dog to grass and then changing your mind two months later is extremely difficult for both dog and owner.

Next, choose the command you will use each and every time

TRAINING TIP
Dogs will do anything for your attention. If you reward the dog when he is calm and resting, you will develop a well-mannered dog. If, on the other hand, you greet your dog excitedly and encourage him to wrestle with you, the dog will greet you the same way and you will have a hyperactive dog on your hands.

you want your puppy to void. 'Hurry up' and 'Toilet' are examples of commands commonly used by dog owners.

Get in the habit of giving the puppy your chosen relief command before you take him out. That way, when he becomes an adult, you will be able to determine if he wants to go out when you ask him. A confirmation will be signs of interest, wagging his tail, watching you intently, going to the door, etc.

PUPPY'S NEEDS
Puppy needs to relieve himself after play periods, after each meal,

All puppies respond naturally to crate training. It is only humans who do not understand a dog's need for 'a den to call his own.'

PARENTAL GUIDANCE
Training a dog is a life experience.
Many parents admit that much of
what they know about raising
children they learned from caring
for their dogs. Dogs respond to love,
fairness and guidance, just as
children do. Become a good dog
owner and you may become an even
better parent.

ately after sleeping and eating.
The older the puppy, the less
often he will need to relieve
himself. Finally, as a mature
healthy adult, he will require only
three to five relief trips per day.

HOUSING
Since the types of housing and
control you provide for your
puppy have a direct relationship
on the success of house-training,
we consider the various aspects of
both before we begin training.

Taking a new puppy home
and turning him loose in your
house can be compared to turning
a child loose in a sports arena and
telling the child that the place is
all his! The sheer enormity of the
place would be too much for him
to handle.

Instead, offer the puppy
clearly defined areas where he can
play, sleep, eat and live. A room
of the house where the family
gathers is the most obvious
choice. Puppies are social animals
and need to feel a part of the pack
right from the start. Hearing your
voice, watching you while you are
doing things and smelling you
nearby are all positive reinforcers
that he is now a member of your
pack. Usually a family room, the
kitchen or a nearby adjoining
breakfast area is ideal for
providing safety and security for
both puppy and owner.

Within that room there should
be a smaller area that the puppy

after he has been sleeping and at
any time he indicates that he is
looking for a place to urinate or
defecate.

The urinary and intestinal
tract muscles of very young
puppies are not fully developed.
Therefore, like human babies,
puppies need to relieve
themselves frequently.

Take your puppy out often—
every hour for an eight-week-old,
for example, and always immedi-

CANINE DEVELOPMENT SCHEDULE

It is important to understand how and at what age a puppy develops into adulthood. If you are a puppy owner, consult the following Canine Development Schedule to determine the stage of development your puppy is currently experiencing. This knowledge will help you as you work with the puppy in the weeks and months ahead.

Period	Age	Characteristics
First to Third	Birth to Seven Weeks	Puppy needs food, sleep and warmth, and responds to simple and gentle touching. Needs mother for security and disciplining. Needs littermates for learning and interacting with other dogs. Pup learns to function within a pack and learns pack order of dominance. Begin socialising with adults and children for short periods. Begins to become aware of its environment.
Fourth	Eight to Twelve Weeks	Brain is fully developed. Needs socialising with outside world. Remove from mother and littermates. Needs to change from canine pack to human pack. Human dominance necessary. Fear period occurs between 8 and 12 weeks. Avoid fright and pain.
Fifth	Thirteen to Sixteen Weeks	Training and formal obedience should begin. Less association with other dogs, more with people, places, situations. Period will pass easily if you remember this is pup's change-to-adolescence time. Be firm and fair. Flight instinct prominent. Permissiveness and over-disciplining can do permanent damage. Praise for good behaviour.
Juvenile	Four to Eight Months	Another fear period about 7 to 8 months of age. It passes quickly, but be cautious of fright and pain. Sexual maturity reached. Dominant traits established. Dog should understand sit, down, come and stay by now.

Note: These are approximate time frames. Allow for individual differences in puppies.

can call his own. An alcove, a wire or fibreglass dog crate or a fenced (not boarded!) corner from which he can view the activities of his new family will be fine. The size of the area or crate is the key factor here. The area must be large

TAKE THE LEAD

Do not carry your dog to his toilet area. Lead him there on a leash or, better yet, encourage him to follow you to the spot. If you start carrying him to his spot, you might end up doing this routine forever and your dog will have the satisfaction of having trained YOU.

MEALTIME

Mealtime should be a peaceful time for your puppy. Do not put his food and water bowls in a high-traffic area in the house. For example, give him his own little corner of the kitchen where he can eat undisturbed and where he will not be underfoot. Do not allow small children or other family members to disturb the pup when he is eating.

enough for the puppy to lie down and stretch out as well as stand up without rubbing his head on the top, yet small enough so that he cannot relieve himself at one end and sleep at the other without coming into contact with his droppings until fully trained to relieve himself outside.

Dogs are, by nature, clean animals and will not remain close to their relief areas unless forced to do so. In those cases, they then become dirty dogs and usually remain that way for life.

The designated area should contain clean bedding and a toy. Water must always be available, in a non-spill container.

CONTROL

By control, we mean helping the puppy to create a lifestyle pattern that will be compatible to that of his human pack (YOU!). Just as we guide little children to learn our way of life, we must show the puppy when it is time to play, eat, sleep, exercise and even entertain himself.

Your puppy should always sleep in his crate. He should also learn that, during times of household confusion and excessive human activity such as at breakfast when family members are preparing for the day, he can play by himself in relative safety and comfort in his designated area. Each time you leave the puppy alone, he should understand exactly where he is to stay. Puppies are chewers. They cannot tell the difference between lamp cords, television wires, shoes, table legs, etc. Chewing into a television wire, for example, can be fatal to the puppy while a shorted wire can start a fire in the house.

If the puppy chews on the arm of the chair when he is alone, you will probably discipline him

COMMAND STANCE
Stand up straight and authoritatively when giving your dog commands. Do not issue commands when lying on the floor or lying on your back on the sofa. If you are on your hands and knees when you give a command, your dog will think you are positioning yourself to play.

angrily when you get home. Thus, he makes the association that your coming home means he is going to be punished. (He will not remember chewing the chair and is incapable of making the association of the discipline with his naughty deed.)

Other times of excitement, such as family parties, etc., can be fun for the puppy providing he can view the activities from the security of his designated area. He is not underfoot and he is not being fed all sorts of titbits that will probably cause him stomach distress, yet he still feels a part of the fun.

THE GOLDEN RULE
The golden rule of dog training is simple. For each 'question' (command), there is only one correct answer (reaction). One command = one reaction. Keep practising the command until the dog reacts correctly without hesitating. Be repetitive but not monotonous. Dogs get bored just as people do!

SCHEDULE

A puppy should be taken to his relief area each time he is released from his designated area, after meals, after a play session and when he first awakens in the morning (at age eight weeks, this can mean 5 a.m.!). The puppy will indicate that he's ready 'to go' by circling or sniffing busily—do not

misinterpret these signs. For a puppy less than ten weeks of age, a routine of taking him out every hour is necessary. As the puppy grows, he will be able to wait for longer periods of time.

Keep trips to his relief area short. Stay no more than five or six minutes and then return to the house. If he goes during that time, praise him lavishly and take him indoors immediately. If he does not, but he has an accident when you go back indoors, pick him up immediately, say 'No! No!' and return to his relief area. Wait a few minutes, then return to the house again. Never hit a puppy or rub his face in urine or excrement when he has had an accident!

Once indoors, put the puppy in his crate until you have had time to clean up his accident. Then release him to the family area and watch him more closely than before. Chances are, his accident was a result of your not picking up his signal or waiting

HOW MANY TIMES A DAY?	
AGE	RELIEF TRIPS
To 14 weeks	10
14–22 weeks	8
22–32 weeks	6
Adulthood	4
(dog stops growing)	

These are estimates, of course, but they are a guide to the MINIMUM opportunities a dog should have each day to relieve itself.

too long before offering him the opportunity to relieve himself. Never hold a grudge against the puppy for accidents.

Let the puppy learn that going outdoors means it is time to relieve himself, not play. Once trained, he will be able to play indoors and out and still differentiate between the times for play

THINK BEFORE YOU BARK

Dogs are sensitive to their masters' moods and emotions. Use your voice wisely when communicating with your dog. Never raise your voice at your dog unless you are angry and trying to correct him. 'Barking' at your dog can become as meaningless as 'dogspeak' is to you. Think before you bark!

KEY TO SUCCESS

Success that comes by luck is usually short-lived. Success that comes by well-thought-out proven methods is often more easily achieved and permanent. This is the Success Method. It is designed to give you, the puppy owner, a simple yet proven way to help your puppy develop clean living habits and a feeling of security in his new environment.

versus the times for relief.

Help him develop regular hours for naps, being alone, playing by himself and just resting, all in his crate. Encourage him to entertain himself while you are busy with your activities. Let him learn that having you near is comforting, but it is not your main purpose in life to provide him with undivided attention.

Each time you put a puppy in his own area, use the same command, whatever suits best. Soon he will run to his crate or special area when he hears you say those words.

Crate training provides safety for you, the puppy and the home. It also provides the puppy with a feeling of security, and that helps the puppy achieve self-confidence and clean habits.

THE SUCCESS METHOD

6 Steps to Successful Crate Training

1 Tell the puppy 'Crate time!' and place him in the crate with a small treat (a piece of cheese or half of a biscuit). Let him stay in the crate for five minutes while you are in the same room. Then release him and praise lavishly. Never release him when he is fussing. Wait until he is quiet before you let him out.

2 Repeat Step 1 several times a day.

3 The next day, place the puppy in the crate as before. Let him stay there for ten minutes. Do this several times.

4 Continue building time in five-minute increments until the puppy stays in his crate for 30 minutes with you in the room. Always take him to his relief area after prolonged periods in his crate.

5 Now go back to Step 1 and let the puppy stay in his crate for five minutes, this time while you are out of the room.

6 Once again, build crate time in five-minute increments with you out of the room. When the puppy will stay willingly in his crate (he may even fall asleep!) for 30 minutes with you out of the room, he will be ready to stay in it for several hours at a time.

PRACTICE MAKES PERFECT!
- Have training lessons with your dog every day in several short segments—three to five times a day for a few minutes at a time is ideal.
- Do not have long practice sessions. The dog will become easily bored.
- Never practise when you are tired, ill, worried or in an otherwise negative mood. This will transmit to the dog and may have an adverse effect on its performance.

    Think fun, short and above all POSITIVE! End each session on a high note, rather than a failed exercise, and make sure to give a lot of praise. Enjoy the training and help your dog enjoy it, too.

Remember that one of the primary ingredients in house-training your puppy is control. Regardless of your lifestyle, there will always be occasions when you will need to have a place where your dog can stay and be happy and safe. Crate training is the answer for now and in the future.

In conclusion, a few key elements are really all you need for a successful house-training method—consistency, frequency, praise, control and supervision. By following these procedures

with a normal, healthy puppy, you and the puppy will soon be past the stage of 'accidents' and ready to move on to a full and rewarding life together.

ROLES OF DISCIPLINE, REWARD AND PUNISHMENT

Discipline, training one to act in accordance with rules, brings order to life. It is as simple as that. Without discipline, particularly in a group society, chaos reigns supreme and the group will eventually perish. Humans and canines are social animals and need some form of discipline in order to function effectively. They must procure food, protect their home base and their young and reproduce to keep the species going.

'NO' MEANS 'NO!'
Dogs do not understand our language. They can be trained to react to a certain sound, at a certain volume. If you say 'No, Oliver' in a very soft pleasant voice it will not have the same meaning as 'No, Oliver!!' when you shout it as loud as you can. You should never use the dog's name during a reprimand, just the command NO!!

Since dogs don't understand words, comics often use dogs trained with opposite meanings. Thus, when the comic commands his dog to SIT the dog will stand up, and vice versa.

TRAINING RULES

If you want to be successful in training your dog, you have four rules to obey yourself:

1. Develop an understanding of how a dog thinks.
2. Do not blame the dog for lack of communication.
3. Define your dog's personality and act accordingly.
4. Have patience and be consistent.

If there were no discipline in the lives of social animals, they would eventually die from starvation and/or predation by other stronger animals.

In the case of domestic canines, dogs need discipline in their lives in order to understand how their pack (you and other family members) functions and how they must act in order to survive.

A large humane society in a highly populated area recently surveyed dog owners regarding their satisfaction with their relationships with their dogs. People who had trained their dogs were 75% more satisfied with their pets than those who had never trained their dogs.

Dr Edward Thorndike, a psychologist, established *Thorndike's Theory of Learning*, which states that a behaviour that results in a pleasant event tends to be repeated. A behaviour that results in an unpleasant event tends not to be repeated. It is this theory on which most training methods are based today. For example, if you manipulate a dog to perform a specific behaviour and reward him for doing it, he is likely to

PLAN TO PLAY

The puppy should also have regular play and exercise sessions when he is with you or a family member. Exercise for a very young puppy can consist of a short walk around the house or garden. Playing can include fetching games with a large ball or a special raggy. (All puppies teethe and need soft things upon which to chew.) Remember to restrict play periods to indoors within his living area (the family room, for example) until he is completely house-trained.

do it again because he enjoyed the end result.

Occasionally, punishment, a penalty inflicted for an offence, is necessary. The best type of punishment often comes from an outside source. For example, a child is told not to touch the stove because he may get burned. He disobeys and touches the stove. In doing so, he receives a burn. From that time on, he respects the heat of the stove and avoids contact with it. Therefore, a behaviour that results in an unpleasant event tends not to be repeated.

A good example of a dog learning the hard way is the dog who chases the house cat. He is told many times to leave the cat alone, yet he persists in teasing the cat. Then, one day he begins chasing the cat but the cat turns and swipes a claw across the dog's face, leaving him with a painful gash on his nose. The final result is that the dog stops chasing the cat.

TRAINING EQUIPMENT

COLLAR AND LEAD
For a Cardigan Welsh Corgi, the collar and lead that you use for training must be one with which you are easily able to work, not too heavy for the dog and perfectly safe.

TREATS
Have a bag of treats on hand. Something nutritious and easy to swallow works best. Use a soft treat, a chunk of cheese or a piece of cooked chicken rather than a dry biscuit. By the time

Be sure your puppy's collar fits properly, without being too loose or too snug.

KEEP SMILING

Never train your dog, puppy or adult, when you are angry or in a sour mood. Dogs are very sensitive to human feelings, especially anger, and if your dog senses that you are angry or upset, he will connect your anger with his training and learn to resent or fear his training sessions.

the dog has finished chewing a dry treat, he will forget why he is being rewarded in the first place! Using food rewards will not teach a dog to beg at the table—the only way to teach a dog to beg at the table is to give him food from the table. In training, rewarding the dog with a food treat will help him associate praise and the treats with

THE CLEAN LIFE

By providing sleeping and resting quarters that fit the dog, and offering frequent opportunities to relieve himself outside his quarters, the puppy quickly learns that the outdoors (or the newspaper if you are training him to paper) is the place to go when he needs to urinate or defecate. It also reinforces his innate desire to keep his sleeping quarters clean. This, in turn, helps develop the muscle control that will eventually produce a dog with clean living habits.

OPEN MINDS

Dogs are as different from each other as people are. What works for one dog may not work for another. Have an open mind. If one method of training is unsuccessful, try another.

learning new behaviours that obviously please his owner.

TRAINING BEGINS: ASK THE DOG A QUESTION

In order to teach your dog anything, you must first get his attention. After all, he cannot learn anything if he is looking away from you with his mind on something else.

To get his attention, ask him, 'School?' and immediately walk over to him and give him a treat as you tell him 'Good dog.' Wait a

you. As he reaches you, give him the treat and praise again.

By this time, the dog will probably be getting the idea that if he pays attention to you, especially when you ask that question, it will pay off in treats and enjoyable activities for him. In other words, he learns that 'school' means doing great things with you that are fun and result in positive attention for him.

Remember that the dog does not understand your verbal language; he only recognises sounds. Your question translates to a series of sounds for him, and those sounds become the signal to go to you and pay attention; if he does, he will get to interact with you plus receive treats and praise.

THE BASIC COMMANDS

TEACHING SIT

Now that you have the dog's attention, attach his lead and hold it in your left hand and a food treat in your right. Place your food hand at the dog's nose and let him lick the treat but not take it from you. Say 'Sit' and slowly raise your food hand from in front of the dog's nose up over his head so that he is looking at the ceiling. As he bends his head upward, he will have to bend his knees to maintain his balance. As he bends his knees, he will assume a sit position. At that point, release the food treat and praise lavishly with

minute or two and repeat the routine, this time with a treat in your hand as you approach within a foot of the dog. Do not go directly to him, but stop about a foot short of him and hold out the treat as you ask, 'School?' He will see you approaching with a treat in your hand and most likely begin walking toward you. As you meet, give him the treat and praise again.

The third time, ask the question, have a treat in your hand and walk only a short distance toward the dog so that he must walk almost all the way to

comments such as 'Good dog! Good sit!,' etc. Remember to always praise enthusiastically, because dogs relish verbal praise from their owners and feel so proud of themselves whenever they accomplish a behaviour.

You will not use food forever in getting the dog to obey your commands. Food is only used to teach new behaviours, and once the dog knows what you want when you give a specific command, you will wean him off the food treats but still maintain the verbal praise. After all, you will always have your voice with you, and there will be many times when you have no food rewards but expect the dog to obey.

FEAR AGGRESSION

Pups who are subjected to physical abuse during training commonly end up with behavioural problems as adults. One common result of abuse is fear aggression, in which a dog will lash out, bare his teeth, snarl and finally bite someone by whom he feels threatened. For example, your daughter may be playing with the dog one afternoon. As they play hide-and-seek, she backs the dog into a corner and, as she attempts to tease him playfully, he bites her hand. Examine the cause of this behaviour. Did your daughter ever hit the dog? Did someone who resembles your daughter hit or scream at the dog?

Fortunately, fear aggression is relatively easy to correct. Have your daughter engage in only positive activities with the dog, such as feeding, petting and walking. She should not give any corrections or negative feedback. If the dog still growls or cowers away from her, allow someone else to accompany them. After approximately one week, the dog should feel that he can rely on her for many positive things, and he will also be prevented from reacting fearfully towards anyone who might resemble her.

TEACHING DOWN

Teaching the down exercise is easy when you understand how the dog perceives the down position, and it is very difficult when you do not. Dogs perceive the down position as a submissive one, therefore teaching the down exercise using a forceful method can sometimes make the dog develop such a fear of the down that he either runs away when you say 'Down' or he attempts to snap at the person who tries to force him down. Fortunately, most Cardis are more comfortable in the down position than are most higher-stationed dogs.

Have the dog sit close alongside your left leg, facing in the same direction as you are. Hold the lead in your left hand and a food treat in your right. Now place your left hand lightly on the top of the dog's shoulders

DOUBLE JEOPARDY

A dog in jeopardy never lies down. He stays alert on his feet because instinct tells him that he may have to run away or fight for his survival. Therefore, if a dog feels threatened or anxious, he will not lie down. Consequently, it is important to have the dog calm and relaxed as he learns the down exercise.

where they meet above the spinal cord. Do not push down on the dog's shoulders; simply rest your left hand there so you can guide the dog to lie down close to your left leg rather than to swing away from your side when he drops.

Now place the food hand at the dog's nose, say 'Down' very softly (almost a whisper), and slowly lower the food hand to the dog's front feet. When the food hand reaches the floor, begin moving it forward along the floor in front of the dog. Keep talking softly to the dog, saying things like, 'Do you want this treat? You can do this, good dog.' Your reassuring tone of voice will help calm the dog as he tries to follow the food hand in order to get the treat.

When the dog's elbows touch the floor, release the food and praise softly. Try to get the dog to maintain that down position for several seconds before you let him sit up again. The goal here is to get the dog to settle down and not feel threatened in the down position.

TEACHING STAY

It is easy to teach the dog to stay in either a sit or a down position. Again, we use food and praise during the teaching process as we help the dog to understand exactly what it is that we are expecting him to do.

To teach the sit/stay, start with the dog sitting on your left side as before and hold the lead in your left hand. Have a food treat in your right hand and place your food hand at the dog's nose. Say 'Stay' and step out on your right foot to stand directly in front of the dog, toe to toe, as he licks and nibbles the treat. Be sure to keep his head facing upward to maintain the sit position. Count to five and then swing around to stand next to the dog again with him on your left. As soon as you get back to the original position, release the food and praise lavishly.

To teach the down/stay, do the down as previously described. As soon as the dog lies down, say 'Stay' and step out on your right foot just as you did in the sit/stay. Count to five and then return to stand beside the dog with him on your left side. Release the treat and praise as always.

Within a week or ten days, you can begin to add a bit of distance between you and your dog when you leave him. When you do, use your left hand open with the palm facing the dog as a stay signal, much the same as the hand signal a constable uses to stop traffic at an intersection. Hold the food treat in your right hand as before, but this time the food is not touching the dog's nose. He will watch the food hand and quickly learn that he is going to get that treat as soon as you return to his side.

When you can stand 1 metre away from your dog for 30 seconds, you can then begin building time and distance in both stays. Eventually, the dog can be expected to remain in the stay position for prolonged periods of time until you return to him or call him to you. Always praise lavishly when he stays.

TEACHING COME

If you make teaching 'come' an exciting experience, you should never have a 'student' that does not love the game or that fails to come when called. The secret, it seems, is never to teach the word 'come.'

At times when an owner most wants his dog to come when called, the owner is likely to be upset or anxious and he allows these feelings to come through in the tone of his voice when he calls his dog. Hearing that desperation in his owner's voice, the dog fears the results of going to him and therefore either disobeys outright or runs in the opposite direction. The secret, therefore, is to teach the dog a game and, when you want him to come to you, simply play the game. It is practically a no-fail solution!

To begin, have several members of your family take a few food treats and each go into a different room in the house. Take turns calling the dog, and each person should celebrate the dog's finding him with a treat and lots of happy praise. When a person calls the dog, he is actually inviting the dog to find him and get a treat as a reward for 'winning.'

A few turns of the 'Where are

you?' game and the dog will understand that everyone is playing the game and that each person has a big celebration awaiting his success at locating him. Once the dog learns to love the game, simply calling out 'Where are you?' will bring him running from wherever he is when he hears that all-important question.

The come command is recognised as one of the most important things to teach a dog, but there are trainers who work with thousands of dogs and never teach the actual word 'Come.' Yet these dogs will race to respond to a person who uses the dog's name followed by 'Where are you?' For example, a woman has a 12-year-old companion dog who went blind, but who never fails to locate her owner when asked, 'Where are you?'

Children, in particular, love to play this game with their dogs. Children can hide in smaller places like a shower or bath, behind a bed or under a table. The dog needs to work a little bit harder to find these hiding places, but when he does he loves to celebrate with a treat and a tussle with a favourite youngster.

TEACHING HEEL

Heeling means that the dog walks beside the owner without pulling. It takes time and patience on the owner's part to succeed at

> **HEELING WELL**
> Teach your dog to HEEL in an enclosed area. Once you think the dog will obey reliably and you want to attempt advanced obedience exercises such as off-lead heeling, test him in a fenced-in area so he cannot run away.

teaching the dog that he (the owner) will not proceed unless the dog is walking calmly beside him. Pulling out ahead on the lead is definitely not acceptable.

Begin by holding the lead in your left hand as the dog sits beside your left leg. Move the loop end of the lead to your right hand but keep your left hand short on the lead so it keeps the dog in close next to you.

Say 'Heel' and step forward on your left foot. Keep the dog close to you and take three steps. Stop and have the dog sit next to you in what we now call the 'heel position.' Praise verbally, but do not touch the dog. Hesitate a moment and begin again with 'Heel,' taking three steps and stopping, at which point the dog is told to sit again.

Your goal here is to have the dog walk those three steps without pulling on the lead. Once he will walk calmly beside you for three steps without pulling, increase the number of steps you take to five. When he will walk politely beside you while you take five steps, you can increase the length of your walk to ten steps. Keep increasing the length of your stroll until the dog will walk quietly beside you without pulling as long as you want him to heel. When you stop heeling, indicate to the dog that the exercise is over by verbally praising as you pet him and say 'OK, good dog.' The 'OK' is used as a release word, meaning that the exercise is finished and the dog is free to relax.

If you are dealing with a dog who insists on pulling you around, simply 'put on your brakes' and stand your ground until the dog realises that the two of you are not going anywhere until he is beside you and moving at your pace, not his. It may take some time just standing there to convince the dog that you are the leader and you will be the one to decide on the direction and speed of your travel.

Each time the dog looks up at you or slows down to give a slack lead between the two of you, quietly praise him and say, 'Good heel. Good dog.' Eventually, the dog will begin to respond and within a few days he will be walking politely beside you without pulling on the lead. At first, the training sessions should be kept short and very positive; soon the dog will be able to walk nicely with you for increasingly longer distances. Remember also to give the dog free time and the opportunity to run and play when you have finished heel practice.

Buster is a senior Cardi, rescued by Richard and Kathleen Hall. This delightful Cardigan has proven that you can teach old dogs new tricks, as he has performed in obedience, agility and herding events with his new family.

WEANING OFF FOOD IN TRAINING
Food is used in training new behaviours. Once the dog understands what behaviour goes with a specific command, it is time to start weaning him off the food treats. At first, give a treat after each exercise. Then, start to

---

FAMILY TIES
If you have other pets in the home and/or interact often with the pets of friends and other family members, your pup will respond to those pets in much the same manner as you do. It is only when you show fear of or resentment toward another animal that he will act fearful or unfriendly.

give a treat only after every other exercise. Mix up the times when you offer a food reward and the times when you only offer praise so that the dog will never know when he is going to receive both food and praise and when he is going to receive only praise. This is called a variable ratio reward system and it proves successful because there is always the chance that the owner will produce a treat, so the dog never stops trying for that reward. No matter what, ALWAYS give verbal praise.

OBEDIENCE CLASSES

It is a good idea to enrol in an obedience class if one is available in your area. If yours is a show dog, ringcraft classes would be more appropriate. Many areas have dog clubs that offer basic obedience training as well as preparatory classes for obedience competition. There are also local dog trainers who offer similar classes.

At obedience shows, dogs can earn titles at various levels of competition. The beginning levels of competition include basic behaviours such as sit, down, heel, etc. The more advanced levels of competition include jumping, retrieving, scent discrimination and signal work. The advanced levels require a dog and owner to put a lot of time and effort into their training, and the

HELPING PAWS
Your dog may not be the next Lassie, but every pet has the potential to do some tricks well. Identify his natural talents and hone them. Is your dog always happy and upbeat? Teach him to wag his tail or give you his paw on command. Real homebodies can be trained to do household chores, such as carrying dirty washing or retrieving the morning paper.

titles that can be earned at these levels of competition are very prestigious. Many Cardigans have found success in obedience and have earned titles.

OTHER ACTIVITIES FOR LIFE

Whether a dog is trained in the structured environment of a class or alone with his owner at home,

OBEDIENCE SCHOOL
A basic obedience beginner's class usually lasts for six to eight weeks. Dog and owner attend an hour-long lesson once a week and practise for a few minutes, several times a day, each day at home. If done properly, the whole procedure will result in a well-mannered dog and an owner who delights in living with a pet that is eager to please and enjoys doing things with his owner.

there are many activities that can bring fun and rewards to both owner and dog once they have mastered basic control.

If you are interested in participating in organised competition with your Cardigan Welsh Corgi, there are activities other than obedience in which you and your dog can become involved. Cardigan breeders take great pride in maintaining and perpetuating the herding ability of their breed. The herding talents of the breed extend themselves to livestock of all kinds—from fowl to cattle. Cardigan owners arrange and participate in these trials the year 'round. The breed enthusiastically and successfully participates in tracking and agility competition as well.

Agility is a popular sport where dogs run through an obstacle course that includes various jumps, tunnels and other exercises to test the dog's speed and coordination. Mini-agility has been devised by The Kennel Club for small breeds to participate. The events are essentially the same except all obstacles have been reduced in size. The owners run beside their dogs to give commands and to guide them through the course. Although competitive, the focus is on fun— it's fun to do, fun to watch and great exercise.

Of course, there are many activities of a non-competitive

nature that dog and owner can enjoy together. Teaching the Cardigan to help out around the home, in the garden or on the farm provides great satisfaction to both dog and owner. In addition, the dog's help makes life a little easier for his owner and raises his stature as a valued companion to his family. It helps give the dog a purpose by occupying his mind and providing an outlet for his energy.

Hiking is an exciting and healthy activity that the dog can be taught without assistance from more than his owner. The exercise of walking and exploring is good for man and dog alike, and the bond that they develop together is priceless.

Agility trials offer the Cardigan many challenges and rewards. Cardigans love to please their owners and will try most anything to achieve that goal. Be careful not to push the Cardi to 'heights' he cannot achieve.

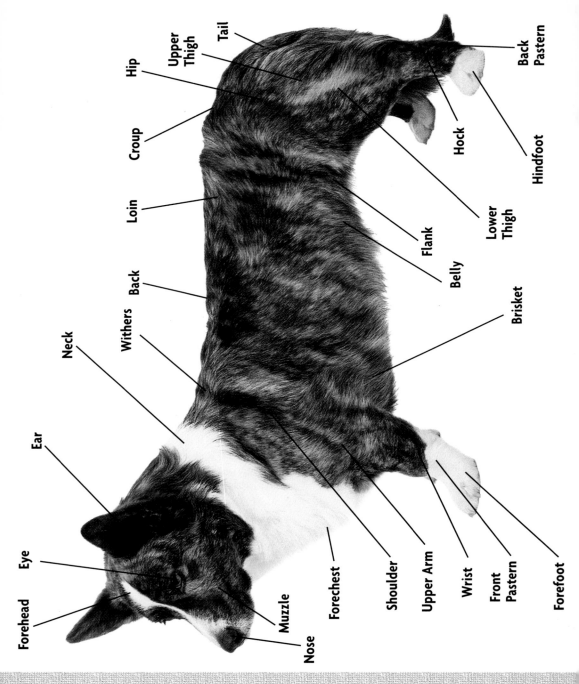

PHYSICAL STRUCTURE OF THE CARDIGAN WELSH CORGI

Dogs suffer from many of the same physical illnesses as people. They might even share many of the same psychological problems. Since people usually know more about human diseases than canine maladies, many of the terms used in this chapter will be familiar but not necessarily those used by veterinary surgeons. We will use the term *x-ray* instead of the more acceptable term *radiograph*. We will also use the familiar term *symptoms* even though dogs don't have symptoms, which are verbal descriptions of the patient's feelings; dogs have *clinical signs*. Since dogs can't speak, we have to look for clinical signs...but we still use the term *symptoms* in this book.

As a general rule, medicine is *practised*. That term is not arbitrary. Medicine is a constantly changing art as we learn more and more about genetics, electronic aids (like CAT scans) and daily laboratory advances. There are many dog maladies, like canine hip dysplasia, which are not universally treated in the same manner. Some veterinary surgeons opt for surgery more often than others do.

SELECTING A VETERINARY SURGEON

Your selection of a veterinary surgeon should not be based upon personality (as most are) but upon his convenience to your home. You want a vet who is close because you might have emergencies or need to make multiple visits for treatments. You want a vet who has services that you might require such as tattooing and grooming, as well as sophisticated pet supplies and a good reputation for ability and responsiveness. There is nothing more frustrating than having to wait a day or more to get a response from your veterinary surgeon.

All veterinary surgeons are licensed and their diplomas and/or certificates should be displayed in their waiting rooms. There are, however, many veterinary specialities that usually require further studies and internships. There are specialists in heart problems (veterinary cardiologists), skin problems (veterinary dermatologists), teeth and gum problems (veterinary dentists), eye problems (veterinary ophthalmologists) and x-rays (veterinary radiologists), as well

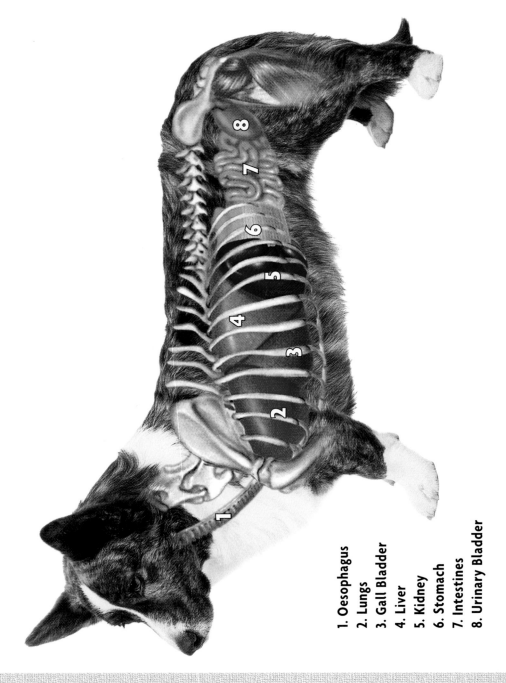

1. Oesophagus
2. Lungs
3. Gall Bladder
4. Liver
5. Kidney
6. Stomach
7. Intestines
8. Urinary Bladder

INTERNAL ORGANS OF THE CARDIGAN WELSH CORGI

as vets who have specialities in bones, muscles or other organs. Most veterinary surgeons do routine surgery such as neutering, stitching up wounds and docking tails for those breeds in which such is required for show purposes. When the problem affecting your dog is serious, it is not unusual or impudent to get another medical opinion, although in Britain you are obliged to advise the vets concerned about this. You might also want to compare costs among several veterinary surgeons. Sophisticated health care and veterinary services can be very costly. It is not infrequent that important decisions are based upon financial considerations.

PREVENTATIVE MEDICINE

It is much easier, less costly and more effective to practise preventative medicine than to fight bouts of illness and disease. Properly bred puppies come from parents who were selected based upon their genetic disease profile. Their mothers should have been vaccinated, free of all internal and external parasites and properly nourished. For these reasons, a visit to the veterinary surgeon who cared for the dam is recommended. The dam can pass on disease resistance to her puppies, which can last for eight to ten weeks. She can also pass on parasites and many infections.

Breakdown of Veterinary Income by Category

2%	Dentistry
4%	Radiology
12%	Surgery
15%	Vaccinations
19%	Laboratory
23%	Examinations
25%	Medicines

That's why you should visit the veterinary surgeon who cared for the dam.

A typical American vet's income categorised according to services performed. This survey dealt with small-animal (pets) practices.

VACCINATION SCHEDULING
Most vaccinations are given by injection and should only be done by a veterinary surgeon. Both he and you should keep a record of the date of the injection, the identification of the vaccine and the amount given. Some vets give a first vaccination at eight weeks, but most dog breeders prefer the course not to commence until about ten weeks because of negating any antibodies passed on by the dam. The vaccination scheduling is usually based on a 15-day cycle. You must take your vet's advice regarding when to vaccinate as this may differ according to the vaccine used. Most vaccinations immunize your puppy against viruses.

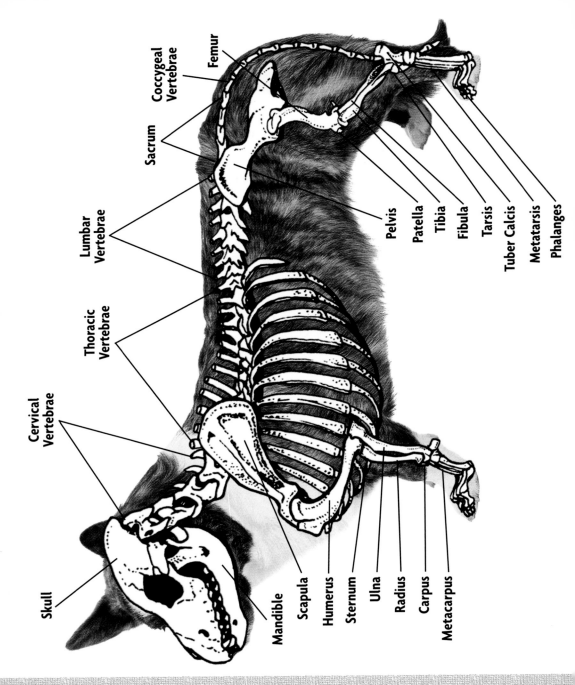

SKELETAL STRUCTURE OF THE CARDIGAN WELSH CORGI

The usual vaccines contain immunizing doses of several different viruses such as distemper, parvovirus, parainfluenza and hepatitis although some veterinary surgeons recommend separate vaccines for each disease. There are other vaccines available when the puppy is at risk. You should rely upon professional advice. This is especially true for the booster-shot programme. Most vaccination programmes require a booster when the puppy is a year old and once a year thereafter. In some cases, circumstances may require more or less frequent immunizations. Kennel cough, more formally known as tracheobronchitis, is treated with a vaccine that is sprayed into the dog's nostrils. Kennel cough is usually included in routine vaccination, but this is often not so effective as for other major diseases.

WEANING TO FIVE MONTHS OLD

Puppies should be weaned by the time they are about two months old. A puppy that remains for at least eight weeks with its mother and littermates usually adapts better to other dogs and people later in its life.

Some new owners have their puppy examined by a veterinary surgeon immediately, which is a good idea. Vaccination programmes usually begin when the puppy is very young.

The puppy will have its teeth examined and have its skeletal conformation and general health checked prior to certification by the veterinary surgeon. Puppies in certain breeds have problems with their kneecaps, cataracts and other eye problems, heart murmurs and undescended testicles. They may also have personality problems and your veterinary surgeon might have training in temperament evaluation.

FIVE TO TWELVE MONTHS OF AGE

Unless you intend to breed or show your dog, neutering the puppy at six months of age is recommended. Discuss this with your veterinary surgeon. Neutering has proven to be extremely beneficial to both male and female puppies. Besides eliminating the possibility of pregnancy, it inhibits (but does not prevent) breast cancer in bitches and prostate cancer in male dogs. Under no circumstances should a bitch be spayed prior to her first season.

Your veterinary surgeon

DID YOU KNOW?

Male dogs are neutered. The operation removes the testicles and requires that the dog be anaesthetised. Recovery takes about one week. Females are spayed. This is major surgery and it usually takes a bitch two weeks to recover.

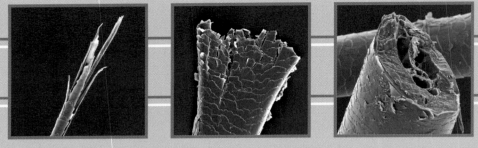

Normal hairs of a dog enlarged 200 times original size. The cuticle (outer covering) is clean and healthy. Unlike human hair that grows from the base, a dog's hair also grows from the end. Damaged hairs and split ends, illustrated above.

should provide your puppy with a thorough dental evaluation at six months of age, ascertaining whether all the permanent teeth have erupted properly. A home dental care regimen should be initiated at six months, including brushing weekly and providing good dental devices (such as nylon bones). Regular dental care promotes healthy teeth, fresh breath and a longer life.

ONE TO SEVEN YEARS

Once a year, your grown dog should visit the vet for an examination and vaccination boosters, if needed. Some vets recommend blood tests, thyroid level check and dental evaluation to accompany these annual visits. A thorough clinical evaluation by the vet can provide critical background information for your dog. Blood tests are often performed at one year of age, and dental examinations around the third or fourth birthday. In the long run, quality preventative care for your pet can save money, teeth and lives.

SKIN PROBLEMS IN CARDIGAN WELSH CORGIS

Veterinary surgeons are consulted by dog owners for skin problems

HEALTH AND VACCINATION SCHEDULE

AGE IN WEEKS:	6TH	8TH	10TH	12TH	14TH	16TH	20-24TH	1 YR
Worm Control	✔	✔	✔	✔	✔	✔	✔	
Neutering								✔
Heartworm		✔		✔		✔	✔	
Parvovirus	✔		✔		✔		✔	✔
Distemper		✔		✔		✔		✔
Hepatitis		✔		✔		✔		✔
Leptospirosis								✔
Parainfluenza	✔		✔		✔			✔
Dental Examination		✔					✔	✔
Complete Physical		✔					✔	✔
Coronavirus				✔			✔	✔
Kennel Cough	✔							
Hip Dysplasia								✔
Rabies							✔	

Vaccinations are not instantly effective. It takes about two weeks for the dog's immune system to develop antibodies. Most vaccinations require annual booster shots. Your veterinary surgeon should guide you in this regard.

more than for any other group of diseases or maladies. Dogs' skin is almost as sensitive as human skin and both suffer almost the same ailments (though the occurrence of acne in dogs is rare!). For this reason, veterinary dermatology has developed into a speciality practised by many veterinary surgeons.

Since many skin problems have visual symptoms that are almost identical, it requires the skill of an experienced veterinary dermatologist to identify and cure many of the more severe skin disorders. Pet shops sell many treatments for skin problems but most of the treatments are directed at symptoms and not the underlying problem(s). If your dog is suffering from a skin disorder, you should seek professional assistance as quickly as possible. As with all diseases, the earlier a problem is identified and treated, the more successful is the cure.

HEREDITARY SKIN DISORDERS
Veterinary dermatologists are currently researching a number of skin disorders that are believed to

Vitamins Recommended for Dogs

Some breeders and vets recommend the supplementation of vitamins to a dog's diet—others do not. Before embarking on a vitamin programme, consult your vet.

Vitamin / Dosage	Food source	Benefits
A / 10,000 IU/week	Eggs, butter, yoghurt, meat	Skin, eyes, hind legs, haircoat
B / Varies	Organs, cottage cheese, sardines	Appetite, fleas, heart, skin and coat
C / 2000 mg+	Fruit, legumes, leafy green vegetables	Healing, arthritis, kidneys
D / Varies	Cod liver, cheese, organs, eggs	Bones, teeth, endocrine system
E / 250 IU daily	Leafy green vegetables, meat, wheat germ oil	Skin, muscles, nerves, healing, digestion
F / Varies	Fish oils, raw meat	Heart, skin, coat, fleas
K / Varies	Naturally in body, not through food	Blood clotting

DISEASE REFERENCE CHART

	What is it?	What causes it?	Symptoms
Leptospirosis	Severe disease that affects the internal organs; can be spread to people.	A bacterium, which is often carried by rodents, that enters through mucous membranes and spreads quickly throughout the body.	Range from fever, vomiting and loss of appetite in less severe cases to shock, irreversible kidney damage and possibly death in most severe cases.
Rabies	Potentially deadly virus that infects warm-blooded mammals. Not seen in United Kingdom.	Bite from a carrier of the virus, mainly wild animals.	1st stage: dog exhibits change in behaviour, fear. 2nd stage: dog's behaviour becomes more aggressive. 3rd stage: loss of coordination, trouble with bodily functions.
Parvovirus	Highly contagious virus, potentially deadly.	Ingestion of the virus, which is usually spread through the faeces of infected dogs.	Most common: severe diarrhoea. Also vomiting, fatigue, lack of appetite.
Kennel cough	Contagious respiratory infection.	Combination of types of bacteria and virus. Most common: *Bordetella bronchiseptica* bacteria and parainfluenza virus.	Chronic cough.
Distemper	Disease primarily affecting respiratory and nervous system.	Virus that is related to the human measles virus.	Mild symptoms such as fever, lack of appetite and mucous secretion progress to evidence of brain damage, 'hard pad.'
Hepatitis	Virus primarily affecting the liver.	Canine adenovirus type I (CAV-1). Enters system when dog breathes in particles.	Lesser symptoms include listlessness, diarrhoea, vomiting. More severe symptoms include 'blue-eye' (clumps of virus in eye).
Coronavirus	Virus resulting in digestive problems.	Virus is spread through infected dog's faeces.	Stomach upset evidenced by lack of appetite, vomiting, diarrhoea.

have an hereditary basis. These inherited diseases are transmitted by both parents, who appear (phenotypically) normal but have a recessive gene for the disease, meaning that they carry, but are not affected by, the disease. These diseases pose serious problems to breeders because in some instances there is no method of identifying carriers. Often the secondary diseases associated with these skin conditions are even more debilitating than the disorder itself, including cancers and respiratory problems; others can be lethal.

Among the hereditary skin disorders, for which the mode of inheritance is known, are acrodermatitis, cutaneous asthenia (Ehlers-Danlos syndrome), sebaceous adenitis, cyclic hematopoiesis, dermatomyositis, IgA deficiency, colour dilution alopecia and nodular dermatofibrosis. Some of these disorders are limited to one or two breeds and others affect a large number of breeds. All inherited diseases must be diagnosed and treated by a veterinary specialist.

Parasite Bites

Many of us are allergic to insect bites. The bites itch, erupt and may even become infected. Dogs have the same reaction to fleas, ticks and/or mites. When an insect lands on you, you have the chance to whisk it away with your hand. Unfortunately, when your dog is bitten by a flea, tick or mite, it can only scratch it away or bite it. By the time the dog has been bitten, the parasite has done some of its damage. It may also have laid eggs to cause further problems in the near future. The itching from parasite bites is probably due to the saliva injected into the site when the parasite sucks the dog's blood.

Auto-Immune Skin Conditions

Auto-immune skin conditions are commonly referred to as being allergic to yourself, while allergies are usually inflammatory reactions to an outside stimulus. Auto-immune diseases cause serious damage to the tissues that are involved.

The best known auto-immune disease is lupus, which affects people as well as dogs. The symptoms are variable and may affect the kidneys, bones, blood chemistry and skin. It can be fatal to both dogs and humans, though it is not thought to be transmissible. It is usually successfully treated with cortisone, prednisone or a similar corticosteroid, but extensive use of these drugs can have harmful side effects.

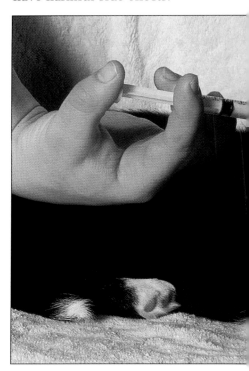

AIRBORNE ALLERGIES

An interesting allergy is pollen allergy. Humans have hay fever, rose fever and other fevers with which they suffer during the pollinating season. Many dogs suffer the same allergies. When the pollen count is high, your dog might suffer but don't expect him to sneeze and have a runny nose like humans. Dogs react to pollen allergies the same way they react to fleas—they scratch and bite themselves.

Dogs, like humans, can be tested for allergens. Discuss the testing with your veterinary dermatologist.

FOOD PROBLEMS

FOOD ALLERGIES

Dogs can be allergic to many foods that are best-sellers and highly recommended by breeders and veterinary surgeons. Changing the brand of food that you buy may not eliminate the problem if the element to which the dog is allergic is also contained in the new brand.

Recognising a food allergy is difficult. Humans vomit or have rashes when they eat a food to which they are allergic. Dogs neither vomit nor (usually) develop a rash. They react in the same manner as they do to an airborne or flea allergy; they itch, scratch and bite, thus making the diagnosis extremely difficult. While pollen allergies and parasite bites are usually seasonal, food allergies are year-round problems.

FOOD INTOLERANCE

Food intolerance is the inability of the dog to completely digest certain foods. Puppies that may have done very well on their mother's milk may not do well when handfed on cow's milk. The result of this food intolerance may be loose bowels, passing gas and stomach pains. These are the only obvious symptoms of food intolerance, thus making a diagnosis difficult.

To protect your Cardi against the major viral diseases, he should be inoculated by your veterinary surgeon. Discuss an inoculation schedule with your vet.

TREATING FOOD PROBLEMS

It is possible to handle food allergies and food intolerance yourself. Put your dog on a diet that it has never had. Obviously if it has never eaten this new food it can't have been allergic or intolerant of it. Start with a single ingredient that is not in the dog's diet at the present time. Ingredients like chopped beef or fish are common in dogs' diets, so try something more exotic like

MORE THAN VACCINES

Vaccinations help prevent your new puppy from contracting diseases, but they do not cure them. Proper nutrition as well as parasite control keep your dog healthy and less susceptible to many dangerous diseases. Remember that your dog depends on you to ensure his well-being.

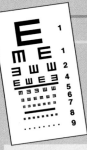

THE EYES HAVE IT!

Eye disease is more prevalent among dogs than most people think, ranging from slight infections that are easily treated to serious complications that can lead to permanent sight loss. Eye diseases need veterinary attention in their early stages to prevent irreparable damage. This list provides descriptions of some common eye diseases:

Cataracts: Symptoms are white or grey discoloration of the eye lens and pupil, which causes fuzzy or completely obscured vision. Surgical treatment is required to remove the damaged lens and replace it with an artificial one.

Conjunctivitis: An inflammation of the mucous membrane that lines the eye socket, leaving the eyes red and puffy with excessive discharge. This condition is easily treated with antibiotics.

Corneal damage: The cornea is the transparent covering of the iris and pupil. Injuries are difficult to detect, but manifest themselves in surface abnormality, redness, pain and discharge. Most infections of the cornea are treated with antibiotics and require immediate medical attention.

Dry eye: This condition is caused by deficient production of tears that lubricate and protect the eye surface. A telltale sign is yellow-green discharge. Left undiagnosed, your dog will experience considerable pain, infections and possibly blindness. Dry eye is commonly treated with antibiotics, although more advanced cases may require surgery.

Glaucoma: This is caused by excessive fluid pressure in the eye. Symptoms are red eyes, grey or blue discoloration, pain, enlarged eyeballs and loss of vision. Antibiotics sometimes help, but surgery may be needed.

rabbit, pheasant or even just vegetables. Keep the dog on this diet (with no additives) for a month. If the symptoms of food allergy or intolerance disappear, chances are your dog has a food allergy.

Don't think that the single ingredient cured the problem. You still must find a suitable diet and ascertain which ingredient in the old diet was objectionable. This is most easily done by adding ingredients to the new diet one at a time. Let the dog stay on the modified diet for a month before you add another ingredient. Eventually, you will determine the ingredient that caused the adverse reaction.

An alternative method is to carefully study the ingredients in the diet to which your dog is

TOXIC PLANTS

Many plants can be toxic to dogs. If you see your dog carrying a piece of vegetation in his mouth, approach him in a quiet, disinterested manner, avoid eye contact, pet him and gradually remove the plant from his mouth. Alternatively, offer him a treat and maybe he'll drop the plant on his own accord. Be sure no toxic plants are growing in your own garden.

VITAL SIGNS

A dog's normal temperature is 38.6° Celcius (101.5° Fahrenheit). A range of between 37.8–39.2° Celcius (100.0 and 102.5° Fahrenheit) should be considered normal, as each dog's body sets its own temperature. It will be helpful if you take your dog's temperature when you know he is healthy and record it. Then, when you suspect that he is not feeling well, you will have a normal figure to compare the abnormal temperature against.

The normal pulse rate for a dog is between 100 and 125 beats per minute.

allergic or intolerant. Identify the main ingredient in this diet and eliminate the main ingredient by buying a different food that does not have that ingredient. Keep experimenting until the symptoms disappear after one month on the new diet.

EXTERNAL PARASITES

FLEAS

Of all the problems to which dogs are prone, none is more well known and frustrating than fleas. Flea infestation is relatively simple to cure but difficult to prevent. Parasites that are harboured inside the body are a bit more difficult to eradicate but they are easier to control.

Magnified head of a dog flea, *Ctenocephalides canis.*

S. E. M. by Dr Dennis Kunkel, University of Hawaii

To control flea infestation, you have to understand the flea's life cycle. Fleas are often thought of as a summertime problem, but centrally heated homes have changed the patterns and fleas can be found at any time of the year. The most effective method of flea control is a two-stage approach: one stage to kill the adult fleas, and the other to control the development of pre-adult fleas. Unfortunately, no single active ingredient is effective against all stages of the life cycle.

LIFE CYCLE STAGES

During its life, a flea will pass through four life stages: egg, larva, pupa and adult. The adult stage is the most visible and irritating stage of the flea life cycle, and this is

Opposite page: A scanning electron micrograph of a dog or cat flea, *Ctenocephalides,* magnified more than 100x. This image has been colorized for effect.

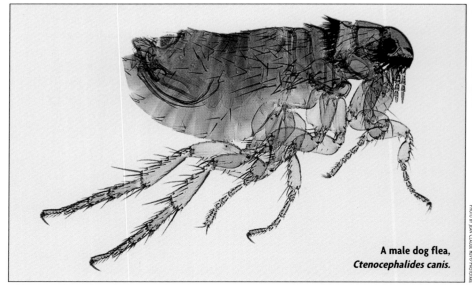

A male dog flea, *Ctenocephalides canis.*

Photo by Jean Claude Revy/Phototake

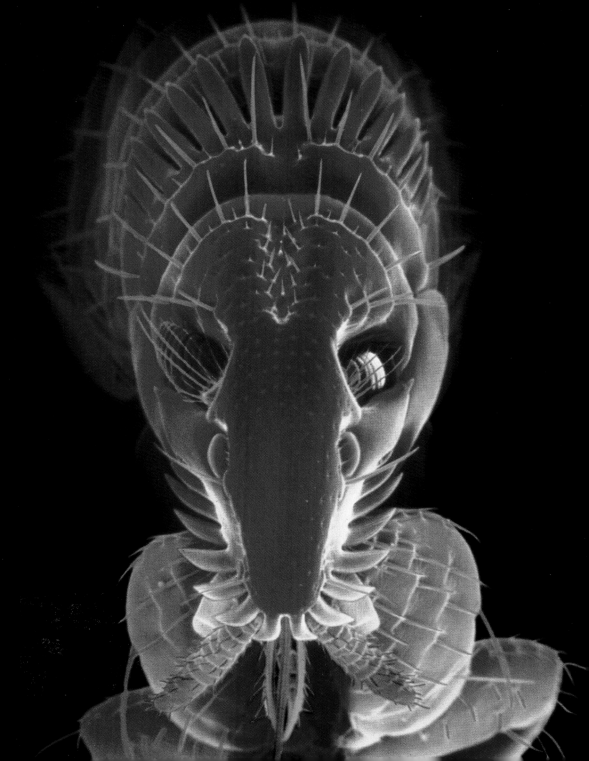

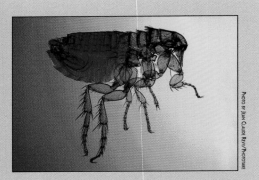

Photo by Jean Claude Revy/Phototake

A LOOK AT FLEAS

Fleas have been around for millions of years and have adapted to changing host animals. They are able to go through a complete life cycle in less than one month or they can extend their lives to almost two years by remaining as pupae or cocoons. They do not need blood or any other food for up to 20 months.

They have been measured as being able to jump 300,000 times and can jump 150 times their length in any direction, including straight up. Those are just a few of the reasons why they are so successful in infesting a dog!

why the majority of flea-control products concentrate on this stage. The fact is that adult fleas account for only 1% of the total flea population, and the other 99% exist in pre-adult stages, i.e. eggs, larvae and pupae. The pre-adult stages are barely visible to the naked eye.

THE LIFE CYCLE OF THE FLEA

Eggs are laid on the dog, usually in quantities of about 20 or 30, several times a day. The female adult flea must have a blood meal before each egg-laying session. When first laid, the eggs will cling to the dog's hair, as the eggs are still moist. However, they will quickly dry out and fall from the dog, especially if the dog moves around or scratches. Many eggs will fall off in the dog's favourite area or an area in which he spends a lot of time, such as his bed.

Once the eggs fall from the dog onto the carpet or furniture, they will hatch into larvae. This takes from one to ten days. Larvae are not particularly mobile and will usually travel only a few inches

The Life Cycle of the Flea

Eggs

Larvae

Pupa

Adult

Photos courtesy of Flea-busters® Rx for Fleas.

FLEA KILLERS

Flea-killers are poisonous. You should not spray these toxic chemicals on areas of a dog's body that he licks, on his genitals or on his face. Flea killers taken internally are a better answer, but check with your vet in case internal therapy is not advised for your dog.

INSECT GROWTH REGULATOR (IGR)

Two types of products should be used when treating fleas—a product to treat the pet and a product to treat the home. Adult fleas represent less than 1% of the flea population. The pre-adult fleas (eggs, larvae and pupae) represent more than 99% of the flea population and are found in the environment; it is in the case of pre-adult fleas that products containing an Insect Growth Regulator (IGR) should be used in the home.

IGRs are a new class of compounds used to prevent the development of insects. They do not kill the insect outright, but instead use the insect's biology against it to stop it from completing its growth. Products that contain methoprene are the world's first and leading IGRs. Used to control fleas and other insects, this type of IGR will stop flea larvae from developing and protect the house for up to seven months.

from where they hatch. However, they do have a tendency to move away from light and heavy traffic—under furniture and behind doors are common places to find high quantities of flea larvae.

The flea larvae feed on dead organic matter, including adult flea faeces, until they are ready to change into adult fleas. Fleas will usually remain as larvae for around seven days. After this period, the larvae will pupate into protective pupae. While inside the pupae, the larvae will undergo metamorphosis and change into adult fleas. This can take as little time as a few days, but the adult fleas can remain inside the pupae waiting to hatch for up to two years. The pupae are signalled to hatch by certain stimuli, such as physical pressure—the pupae's being stepped on, heat from an animal lying on the pupae or increased carbon dioxide levels and vibrations—indicating that a suitable host is available.

Once hatched, the adult flea must feed within a few days. Once the adult flea finds a host, it will not leave voluntarily. It only becomes dislodged by grooming or the host animal's scratching. The adult flea will remain on the host for the duration of its life unless forcibly removed.

PHOTO BY DWIGHT R KUHN

Dwight R Kuhn's magnificent action photo, showing a flea jumping from a dog's back.

TREATING THE ENVIRONMENT AND THE DOG

Treating fleas should be a two-pronged attack. First, the environment needs to be treated; this includes carpets and furniture, especially the dog's bedding and areas underneath furniture. The environment should be treated with a household spray containing an Insect Growth Regulator (IGR) and an insecticide to kill the adult fleas. Most IGRs are effective against eggs and larvae; they

A scanning electron micrograph (S. E. M.) of a dog flea, *Ctenocephalides canis.*

S. E. M. BY DR DENNIS KUNKEL, UNIVERSITY OF HAWAII

actually mimic the fleas' own hormones and stop the eggs and larvae from developing into adult fleas. There are currently no treatments available to attack the pupa stage of the life cycle, so the adult insecticide is used to kill the newly hatched adult fleas before they find a host. Most IGRs are active for many months, while adult insecticides are only active for a few days.

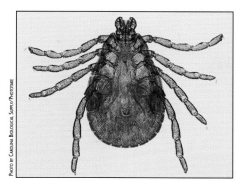

A brown dog tick, *Rhipicephalus sanguineus*, is an uncommon but annoying tick found on dogs.

DID YOU KNOW?

Never mix flea control products without first consulting your veterinary surgeon. Some products can become toxic when combined with others and can cause serious or fatal consequences.

When treating with a household spray, it is a good idea to vacuum before applying the product. This stimulates as many pupae as possible to hatch into adult fleas. The vacuum cleaner should also be treated with an insecticide to prevent the eggs and larvae that have been hoovered into the vacuum bag from hatching.

The second stage of treatment is to apply an adult insecticide to the dog. Traditionally, this would be in the form of a collar or a spray, but more recent innovations include digestible insecticides that poison the fleas when they ingest the dog's blood. Alternatively, there are drops that, when placed on the back of the animal's neck, spread throughout the fur and skin to kill adult fleas.

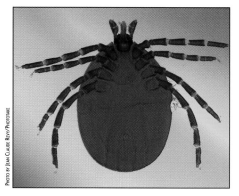

An uncommon dog tick of the genus *Ixode*. Magnified 10x.

TICKS AND MITES

Though not as common as fleas, ticks and mites are found all over the tropical and temperate world. They don't bite, like fleas; they harpoon. They dig their sharp proboscis (nose) into the dog's skin and drink the blood. Their only food and drink is dog's blood. Dogs can get Lyme disease, Rocky Mountain spotted fever (normally found in the US only), paralysis and many other diseases from ticks and mites. They may live where fleas are

The head of a dog tick, *Dermacentor variabilis*, enlarged and coloured for effect.

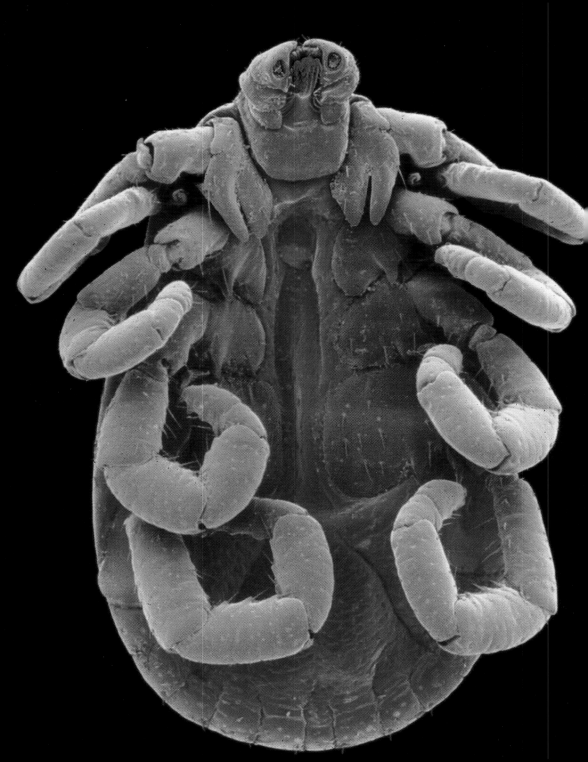

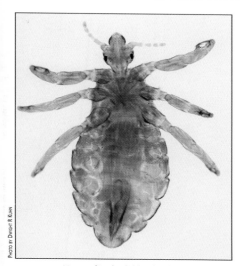

PHOTO BY DWIGHT R KUHN

Human lice look like dog lice; the two are closely related.

S. E. M. BY DR ANDREW SPIELMAN/PHOTOTAKE

BEWARE THE DEER TICK

The great outdoors may be fun for your dog, but it also is a home to dangerous ticks. Deer ticks carry a bacterium known as *Borrelia burgdorferi* and are most active in the autumn and spring. When infections are caught early, penicillin and tetracycline are effective antibiotics, but if left untreated the bacteria may cause neurological, kidney and cardiac problems as well as long-term trouble with walking and painful joints.

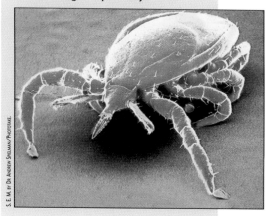

found and they like to hide in cracks or seams in walls wherever dogs live. They are controlled the same way fleas are controlled.

The dog tick, *Dermacentor variabilis*, may well be the most common dog tick in many geographical areas, especially those areas where the climate is hot and humid.

Most dog ticks have life expectancies of a week to six months, depending upon climatic conditions. They can neither jump nor fly, but they

Opposite page:
The dog tick, *Dermacentor variabilis*, is probably the most common tick found on dogs. Look at the strength in its eight legs! No wonder it's hard to detach them.

can crawl slowly and can range up to 5 metres (16 feet) to reach a sleeping or unsuspecting dog.

MANGE

Mites cause a skin irritation called mange. Some are contagious, like *Cheyletiella*, ear mites, scabies and chiggers. Mites that cause ear-mite infestations are usually controlled with Lindane, which can only be

The mange mite, *Psoroptes bovis.*

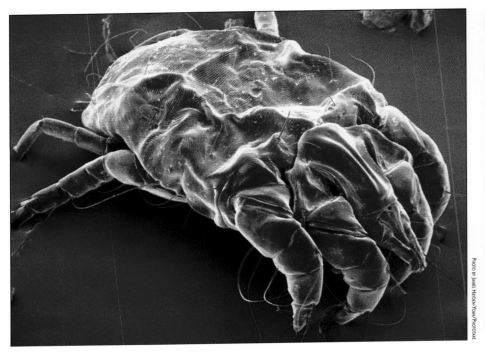

PHOTO BY JAMES HAYDEN-YOAV/PHOTOTAKE

The roundworm, *Rhabditis.* The roundworm can infect both dogs and humans.

PHOTO BY CAROLINA BIOLOGICAL SUPPLY/PHOTOTAKE

The common roundworm, *Ascaris lumbricoides.*

PHOTO BY DWIGHT R. KUHN

administered by a vet, followed by Tresaderm at home.

It is essential that your dog be treated for mange as quickly as possible because some forms of mange are transmissible to people.

INTERNAL PARASITES

Most animals—fishes, birds and mammals, including dogs and humans—have worms and other parasites that live inside their bodies. According to Dr Herbert R Axelrod, the fish pathologist, there are two kinds of parasites: dumb and smart. The smart parasites live in peaceful cooperation with their hosts (symbiosis), while the dumb parasites kill their hosts. Most of the worm infections are relatively easy to control. If they are not controlled, they weaken the host dog to the point that other medical problems occur, but they are not dumb parasites.

ROUNDWORMS

The roundworms that infect dogs are scientifically known as *Toxocara canis*. They live in the dog's intestines. The worms shed eggs continually. It has been estimated that a dog produces about 150 grammes of faeces every day. Each gramme of faeces

ROUNDWORMS

Average-size dogs can pass 1,360,000 roundworm eggs every day. For example, if there were only 1 million dogs in the world, the world would be saturated with 1,300 metric tonnes of dog faeces. These faeces would contain 15,000,000,000 roundworm eggs.

Up to 31% of home gardens and children's play boxes in the US contain roundworm eggs.

Flushing dog's faeces down the toilet is not a safe practice because the usual sewage treatments do not destroy roundworm eggs.

Infected puppies start shedding roundworm eggs at 3 weeks of age. They can be infected by their mother's milk.

DEWORMING

Ridding your puppy of worms is *very important* because certain worms that puppies carry, such as tapeworms and roundworms, can infect humans.

Breeders initiate deworming programmes at or about four weeks of age. The routine is repeated every two or three weeks until the puppy is three months old. The breeder from whom you obtained your puppy should provide you with the complete details of the deworming programme.

Your veterinary surgeon can prescribe and monitor the programme of deworming for you. The usual programme is treating the puppy every 15–20 days until the puppy is positively worm-free. It is advised that you only treat your puppy with drugs that are recommended professionally.

averages 10,000–12,000 eggs of roundworms. There are no known areas in which dogs roam that do not contain roundworm eggs. The greatest danger of roundworms is that they infect people too! It is wise to have your dog tested regularly for roundworms.

Pigs also have roundworm infections that can be passed to humans and dogs. The typical roundworm parasite is called *Ascaris lumbricoides*.

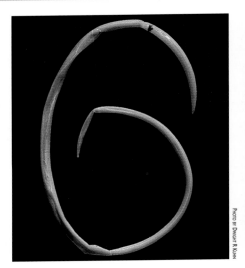

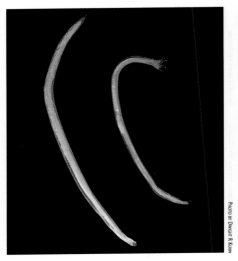

HOOKWORMS

The worm *Ancylostoma caninum* is commonly called the dog hookworm. It is also dangerous to humans and cats. It has teeth by which it attaches itself to the intestines of the dog. It changes the site of its attachment about six times a day and the dog loses blood from each detachment, possibly causing iron-deficiency anaemia. Hookworms are easily purged from the dog with many medications. Milbemycin oxime, which also serves as a heartworm preventative in Collies, can be used for this purpose.

In Britain the 'temperate climate' hookworm (*Uncinaria stenocephala*) is rarely found in pet or show dogs, but can occur in hunting packs, racing Greyhounds and sheepdogs because the worms can be prevalent wherever dogs are exercised regularly on grassland.

TAPEWORMS

There are many species of tapeworm. They are carried by fleas! The dog eats the flea and starts the tapeworm cycle. Humans can also be infected with tapeworms, so don't eat fleas! Fleas are so small that your dog could pass them onto your hands, your plate or your food and thus make it possible for you to ingest a flea that is carrying tapeworm eggs.

While tapeworm infection is

The infective stage of the hookworm larva.

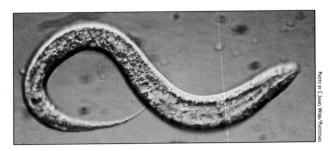

Heartworm, *Dirofilaria immitis.*

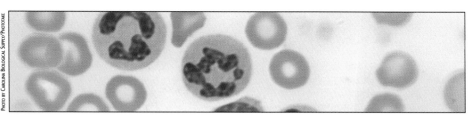

Magnified heartworm larvae, *Dirofilaria immitis.*

not life-threatening in dogs (smart parasite!), it can be the cause of a very serious liver disease for humans. About 50 percent of the humans infected with *Echinococcus multilocularis*, a type of tapeworm that causes alveolar hydatis, perish.

TAPEWORMS

Humans, rats, squirrels, foxes, coyotes, wolves, and domestic dogs are all susceptible to tapeworm infection. Except in humans, tapeworms are usually not a fatal infection. Infected individuals can harbour a thousand parasitic worms.

Tapeworms have two sexes—male and female (many other worms have only one sex—male and female in the same worm).

If dogs eat infected rats or mice, they get the tapeworm disease. One month after attaching to a dog's intestine, the worm starts shedding eggs. These eggs are infective immediately. Infective eggs can live for a few months without a host animal.

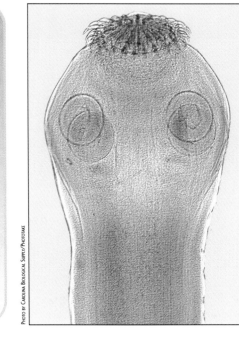

The head and rostellum (the round prominence on the scolex) of a tapeworm, which infects dogs and humans.

The heart of a dog infected with canine heartworm, *Dirofilaria immitis.*

PHOTO BY JAMES E HAYDEN, RPB/PHOTOTAKE

HEARTWORMS

Heartworms are thin, extended worms up to 30 cms (12 ins) long, which live in a dog's heart and the major blood vessels surrounding it. Dogs may have up to 200 worms. Symptoms may be loss of energy, loss of appetite, coughing, the development of a pot belly and anaemia.

Heartworms are transmitted by mosquitoes. The mosquito drinks the blood of an infected dog and takes in larvae with the blood. The larvae, called microfilaria, develop within the body of the mosquito and are passed on to the next dog bitten after the larvae mature. It takes two to three weeks for the larvae to develop to the infective stage within the body of the mosquito. Dogs should be treated at about six weeks of age, and maintained on a prophylactic dose given monthly.

Blood testing for heartworms is not necessarily indicative of how seriously your dog is infected. This is a dangerous disease. Although heartworm is a problem for dogs in America, Australia, Asia and Central Europe, dogs in the United Kingdom are not currently affected by heartworm.

First Aid at a Glance

Burns
Place the affected area under cool water;
use ice if only a small area is burnt.

Bee/Insect bites
Apply ice to relieve swelling;
antihistamine dosed properly.

Animal bites
Clean any bleeding area; apply pressure
until bleeding subsides; go to the vet.

Spider bites
Use cold compress and a pressurised
pack to inhibit venom's spreading.

Antifreeze poisoning
Induce vomiting with hydrogen peroxide.
Seek *immediate* veterinary help!

Fish hooks
Removal best handled by vet;
hook must be cut in order to remove.

Snake bites
Pack ice around bite; contact vet
quickly; identify snake for proper
antivenin.

Car accident
Move dog from roadway with blanket;
seek veterinary aid.

Shock
Calm the dog, keep him warm; seek
immediate veterinary help.

Nosebleed
Apply cold compress to the nose; apply
pressure to any visible abrasion.

Bleeding
Apply pressure above the area; treat
wound by applying a cotton pack.

Heat stroke
Submerge dog in cold bath; cool down
with fresh air and water; go to the vet.

Frostbite/Hypothermia
Warm the dog with a warm bath, electric
blankets or hot water bottles.

Abrasions
Clean the wound and wash out
thoroughly with fresh water;
apply antiseptic.

 *Remember: an injured dog may attempt
to bite a helping hand from fear and confusion.
Always muzzle the dog before trying to offer assistance.*

HOMEOPATHY:
an alternative
to conventional
medicine

'Less is Most'

Using this principle, the strength of a homeopathic remedy is measured by the number of serial dilutions that were undertaken to create it. The greater the number of serial dilutions, the greater the strength of the homeopathic remedy. The potency of a remedy that has been made by making a dilution of 1 part in 100 parts (or 1/100) is 1c or 1cH. If this remedy is subjected to a series of further dilutions, each one being 1/100, a more dilute and stronger remedy is produced. If the remedy is diluted in this way six times, it is called 6c or 6cH. A dilution of 6c is 1 part in 1,000,000,000,000. In general, higher potencies in more frequent doses are better for acute symptoms and lower potencies in more infrequent doses are more useful for chronic, long-standing problems.

CURING OUR DOGS NATURALLY

Holistic medicine means treating the whole animal as a unique, perfect living being. Generally, holistic treatments do not suppress the symptoms that the body naturally produces, as do most medications prescribed by conventional doctors and vets. Holistic methods seek to cure disease by regaining balance and harmony in the patient's environment. Some of these methods include use of nutritional therapy, herbs, flower essences, aromatherapy, acupuncture, massage, chiropractic and, of course, the most popular holistic approach, homeopathy.

Homeopathy is a theory or system of treating illness with small doses of substances which, if administered in larger quantities, would produce the symptoms that the patient already has. This approach is often described as 'like cures like.' Although modern veterinary medicine is geared toward the 'quick fix,' homeopathy relies on the belief that, given the time, the body is able to heal itself and return to its natural, healthy state.

Choosing a remedy to cure a problem in our dogs is the difficult part of homeopathy. Consult with your veterinary surgeon for a professional diagnosis of your dog's symptoms. Often these symptoms require immediate conventional care. If your vet is willing, and knowledgeable, you may attempt a homeopathic remedy. Be aware that cortisone prevents homeopathic remedies from working. There are hundreds of possibilities and combinations to cure many problems in dogs, from basic physical problems such as excessive moulting, fleas or other parasites, unattractive doggy odour, bad breath, upset tummy, obesity, dry, oily or dull coat, diarrhoea, ear problems or eye discharge (including tears and dry or mucousy matter), to behavioural abnormalities, such as fear of loud noises, habitual licking, poor appetite, excessive barking and various phobias. From alumina to zincum metallicum, the remedies span the planet and the imagination…from flowers and weeds to chemicals, insect droppings, diesel smoke and volcanic ash.

Using 'Like to Treat Like'

Unlike conventional medicines that suppress symptoms, homeopathic remedies treat illnesses with small doses of substances that, if administered in larger quantities, would produce the symptoms that the patient already has. While the same homeopathic remedy can be used to treat different symptoms in different dogs, here are some interesting remedies and their uses.

Apis Mellifica
(made from honey bee venom) can be used for allergies or to reduce swelling that occurs in acutely infected kidneys.

Diesel Smoke
can be used to help control travel sickness.

Calcarea Fluorica
(made from calcium fluoride, which helps harden bone structure) can be useful in treating hard lumps in tissues.

Natrum Muriaticum
(made from common salt, sodium chloride) is useful in treating thin, thirsty dogs.

Nitricum Acidum
(made from nitric acid) is used for symptoms you would expect to see from contact with acids, such as lesions, especially where the skin joins the linings of body orifices or openings such as the lips and nostrils.

Symphytum
(made from the herb Knitbone, *Symphytum officianale*) is used to encourage bones to heal.

Urtica Urens
(made from the common stinging nettle) is used in treating painful, irritating rashes.

HOMEOPATHIC REMEDIES FOR YOUR DOG

Symptom/Ailment	Possible Remedy
ALLERGIES	Apis Mellifica 30c, Astacus Fluviatilis 6c, Pulsatilla 30c, Urtica Urens 6c
ALOPAECIA	Alumina 30c, Lycopodium 30c, Sepia 30c, Thallium 6c
ANAL GLANDS (BLOCKED)	Hepar Sulphuris Calcareum 30c, Sanicula 6c, Silicea 6c
ARTHRITIS	Rhus Toxicodendron 6c, Bryonia Alba 6c
CATARACT	Calcarea Carbonica 6c, Conium Maculatum 6c, Phosphorus 30c, Silicea 30c
CONSTIPATION	Alumina 6c, Carbo Vegetabilis 30c, Graphites 6c, Nitricum Acidum 30c, Silicea 6c
COUGHING	Aconitum Napellus 6c, Belladonna 30c, Hyoscyamus Niger 30c, Phosphorus 30c
DIARRHOEA	Arsenicum Album 30c, Aconitum Napellus 6c, Chamomilla 30c, Mercurius Corrosivus 30c
DRY EYE	Zincum Metallicum 30c
EAR PROBLEMS	Aconitum Napellus 30c, Belladonna 30c, Hepar Sulphuris 30c, Tellurium 30c, Psorinum 200c
EYE PROBLEMS	Borax 6c, Aconitum Napellus 30c, Graphites 6c, Staphysagria 6c, Thuja Occidentalis 30c
GLAUCOMA	Aconitum Napellus 30c, Apis Mellifica 6c, Phosphorus 30c
HEAT STROKE	Belladonna 30c, Gelsemium Sempervirens 30c, Sulphur 30c
HICCOUGHS	Cinchona Deficinalis 6c
HIP DYSPLASIA	Colocynthis 6c, Rhus Toxicodendron 6c, Bryonia Alba 6c
INCONTINENCE	Argentum Nitricum 6c, Causticum 30c, Conium Maculatum 30c, Pulsatilla 30c, Sepia 30c
INSECT BITES	Apis Mellifica 30c, Cantharis 30c, Hypericum Perforatum 6c, Urtica Urens 30c
ITCHING	Alumina 30c, Arsenicum Album 30c, Carbo Vegetabilis 30c, Hypericum Perforatum 6c, Mezerium 6c, Sulphur 30c
KENNEL COUGH	Drosera 6c, Ipecacuanha 30c
MASTITIS	Apis Mellifica 30c, Belladonna 30c, Urtica Urens 1m
PATELLAR LUXATION	Gelsemium Sempervirens 6c, Rhus Toxicodendron 6c
PENIS PROBLEMS	Aconitum Napellus 30c, Hepar Sulphuris Calcareum 30c, Pulsatilla 30c, Thuja Occidentalis 6c
PUPPY TEETHING	Calcarea Carbonica 6c, Chamomilla 6c, Phytolacca 6c
TRAVEL SICKNESS	Cocculus 6c, Petroleum 6c

Recognising a Sick Dog

Unlike colicky babies and cranky children, our canine charges cannot tell us when they are feeling ill. Therefore, there are a number of signs that owners can identify to know that their dogs are not feeling well.

**Take note for
physical manifestations such as:**

- unusual, bad odour, including bad breath
- excessive moulting
- wax in the ears, chronic ear irritation
- oily, flaky, dull haircoat
- mucous, tearing or similar discharge in the eyes
- fleas or mites
- mucous in stool, diarrhoea
- sensitivity to petting or handling
- licking at paws, scratching face, etc.

**Keep an eye out for
behavioural changes as well including:**

- lethargy, idleness
- lack of patience or general irritability
- lack of appetite, digestive problems
- phobias (fear of people, loud noises, etc.)
- strange behaviour, suspicion, fear
- coprophagia
- more frequent barking
- whimpering, crying

Get Well Soon

You don't need a DVR or a BVMA to provide good TLC to your sick or recovering dog, but you do need to pay attention to some details that normally wouldn't bother him. The following tips will aid Fido's recovery and get him back on his paws again:

- Keep his space free of irritating smells, like heavy perfumes and air fresheners.
- Rest is the best medicine! Avoid harsh lighting that will prevent your dog from sleeping. Shade him from bright sunlight during the day and dim the lights in the evening.
- Keep the noise level down. Animals are more sensitive to sound when they are sick.

- Be attentive to any necessary temperature adjustments. A dog with a fever needs a cool room and cold liquids. A bitch that is whelping or recovering from surgery will be more comfortable in a warm room, consuming warm liquids and food.
- You wouldn't send a sick child back to school early, so don't rush your dog back into a full routine until he seems absolutely ready.

The term *old* is a qualitative term. For dogs, as well as their masters, old is relative. Certainly we can all distinguish between a puppy Cardigan and an adult Cardigan—there are the obvious physical traits, such as size, appearance and facial expressions, and personality traits. Puppies and young dogs like to play with children. Children's natural exuberance is a good match for the seemingly endless energy of young dogs. They like to run, jump, chase and retrieve. When dogs grow older and cease their interaction with children, they are often thought of as being 'too old to play with the children.'

On the other hand, if a Cardigan is only exposed to people over 60 years of age, its life will normally be less active and it will not seem to be getting old as its activity level slows down.

If people live to be 100 years old, dogs live to be 20 years old. While this is a good rule of thumb, it is very inaccurate. When trying to compare dog years to human years, you cannot make a generalisation about all dogs. You can make the generalisation that 12–14 years is a good lifespan

for a Cardigan, which is quite good compared to many other pure-bred dogs that may only live to 8 or 9 years of age. Dogs are generally considered mature within three years, but they can reproduce even earlier. So the first three years of a dog's life are like seven times that of comparable humans. That means a 3-year-old dog is like a 21-year-old human. As the curve of comparison shows, there is no hard and fast rule for comparing dog and human ages. The comparison is made even more difficult, for not all humans age at the same rate...and human females live longer than human males.

WHAT TO LOOK FOR IN A VETERAN

Most veterinary surgeons and behaviourists use the seventh-year mark as the time to consider a dog a 'veteran' or 'senior.' This does not imply that the dog is geriatric and has begun to fail in mind and body. Ageing is essentially a slowing process. Humans readily admit that they feel a difference in their activity level from age 20 to 30, and then from 30 to 40, etc. By treating the seven-year-old dog as a senior, owners are able to implement certain therapeutic and preventative medical strategies with the help of their veterinary surgeons. A senior-care programme should include at least two veterinary visits per year, screening sessions to determine the dog's health status, as well as nutritional counselling. Veterinary surgeons determine the senior dog's health status through a blood smear for a complete blood count, serum chemistry profile with electrolytes, urinalysis, blood pressure check, electrocardiogram, ocular tonometry (pressure on the eyeball) and dental prophylaxis.

Such an extensive programme for senior dogs is well advised before owners start to see the obvious physical signs of ageing, such as slower and inhibited movement, greying, increased sleep/nap periods and disinterest in play and other activity. This preventative programme promises a longer, healthier life for the ageing dog. Among the physical problems common in ageing dogs are the loss of sight and hearing, arthritis, kidney and liver failure, diabetes mellitus, heart disease, and Cushing's disease (an hormonal disease).

In addition to the physical manifestations discussed, there are some behavioural changes and problems related to ageing dogs. Dogs suffering from hearing or vision loss, dental discomfort or arthritis can become aggressive.

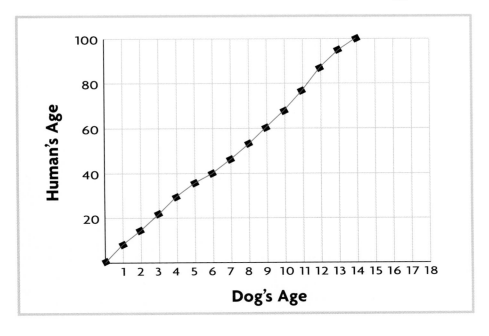

Likewise the near-deaf and/or blind dog may be startled more easily and react in an unexpectedly aggressive manner. Seniors suffering from senility can become more impatient and irritable. Housesoiling accidents are associated with loss of mobility, kidney problems and loss of sphincter control, as well as plaque accumulation, physiological brain changes and reactions to medications. Older dogs, just like young puppies, suffer from separation anxiety, which can lead to excessive barking, whining, housesoiling and destructive behaviour. Seniors may become fearful of everyday sounds, such as vacuum cleaners, heaters, thunder and passing traffic. Some dogs have difficulty sleeping, due to discomfort, the need for frequent toilet visits and the like.

Owners should avoid spoiling the older dog with too many fatty treats. Obesity is a common problem in older dogs and subtracts years from their lives. Keep the senior dog as trim as possible since excessive weight puts additional stress on the body's vital organs. Some breeders recommend supplementing the diet with foods high in fibre and lower in calories. Adding fresh vegetables and marrow broth to the senior's diet makes a tasty, low-calorie, low-fat supplement. Vets also offer speciality diets for senior dogs that are worth exploring.

Your dog, as he nears his twilight years, needs his owner's patience and good care more than ever. Never punish an older dog for an accident or abnormal behaviour. For all the years of love, protection and companionship that your dog has provided, he deserves special attention and courtesies. The older dog may need to relieve himself at 3 a.m. because he can no longer hold it for eight hours. Older dogs may not be able to remain crated for more than two or three hours. It may be time to give up a sofa or chair to your old friend. Although he may not seem as enthusiastic about your attention and petting, he does appreciate the considerations you offer as he gets older.

Your Cardigan does not understand why his world is slowing down. Owners must make the transition into the golden years as pleasant and rewarding as possible.

WHAT TO DO WHEN THE TIME COMES

You are never fully prepared to make a rational decision about putting your dog to sleep. It is very obvious that you love your Cardigan or you would not be reading this book. Putting a loved dog to sleep is extremely difficult. It is a decision that must be made with your veterinary surgeon. You are usually forced to make the

CDS: COGNITIVE DYSFUNCTION SYNDROME
'OLD-DOG SYNDROME'

There are many ways to evaluate old-dog syndrome. Veterinary surgeons have defined CDS (cognitive dysfunction syndrome) as the gradual deterioration of cognitive abilities. These are indicated by changes in the dog's behaviour. When a dog changes its routine response, and maladies have been eliminated as the cause of these behavioural changes, then CDS is the usual diagnosis.

More than half the dogs over eight years old suffer from some form of CDS. The older the dog, the more chance it has of suffering from CDS. In humans, doctors often dismiss the CDS behavioural changes as part of 'winding down.'

There are four major signs of CDS: the dog has frequent toilet accidents inside the home, sleeps much more or much less than normal, acts confused and fails to respond to social stimuli.

SYMPTOMS OF CDS

FREQUENT TOILET ACCIDENTS
- *Urinates in the house.*
- *Defecates in the house.*
- *Doesn't signal that he wants to go out.*

SLEEP PATTERNS
- *Moves much more slowly.*
- *Sleeps more than normal during the day.*
- *Sleeps less during the night.*

CONFUSION
- *Goes outside and just stands there.*
- *Appears confused with a faraway look in his eyes.*
- *Hides more often.*
- *Doesn't recognise friends.*
- *Doesn't come when called.*
- *Walks around listlessly and without a destination.*

FAILS TO RESPOND TO SOCIAL STIMULI
- *Comes to people less frequently, whether called or not.*
- *Doesn't tolerate petting for more than a short time.*
- *Doesn't come to the door when you return home.*

There are cemeteries for deceased pets. Consult with your veterinary surgeon to help find one in your area.

decision when one of the life-threatening symptoms listed above becomes serious enough for you to seek medical (veterinary) help.

If the prognosis of the malady indicates the end is near and your beloved pet will only suffer more and experience no enjoyment for the balance of its life, then euthanasia is the right choice.

WHAT IS EUTHANASIA?

Euthanasia derives from the Greek, meaning *good death*. In other words, it means the planned, painless killing of a dog suffering from a painful, incurable condition, or who is so aged that it cannot walk, see, eat or control its excretory functions.

Euthanasia is usually accomplished by injection with an overdose of an anaesthesia or barbiturate. Aside from the prick of the needle, the experience is usually painless.

MAKING THE DECISION

The decision to euthanise your dog is never easy. The days during which the dog becomes ill and the end occurs can be unusually stressful for you. If this is your first experience with the death of a loved one, you may need the comfort dictated by your religious beliefs. If you are the head of the family and have children, you should have involved them in the decision of putting your Cardigan to sleep. Usually your dog can be maintained on drugs for a few days in order to give you ample time to make a decision. During this time, talking with members of your family or even people who have lived through this same experience can ease the burden of your inevitable decision.

THE FINAL RESTING PLACE

Dogs can have some of the same privileges as humans. The remains of your beloved dog can be buried in a pet cemetery, which is generally expensive. Dogs who have died at home can be buried in your garden in a place suitably marked with some stone or newly planted tree or bush. Alternatively, they can be cremated individually and the ashes returned to you. A less expensive option is mass cremation, although, of course, the ashes can not then be returned. Vets can usually arrange the cremation on your behalf. The cost of these options should always be discussed frankly and openly with your veterinary surgeon. In Britain if your dog has died at the surgery the vet legally cannot allow you to take your dog's body home.

Cremation is an option for those who wish to memorialise their deceased pets. Cemeteries usually have areas to accommodate urns that contain the dogs' ashes.

GETTING ANOTHER DOG?

The grief of losing your beloved dog will be as lasting as the grief of losing a human friend or relative. In most cases, if your dog died of old age (if there is such a thing), it had slowed down considerably. Do you want a new Cardigan puppy to replace it? Or are you better off finding a more mature Cardigan, say two to three years of age, which will usually be house-trained and will have an already developed personality. In this case, you can find out if you like each other after a few hours of being together.

The decision is, of course, your own. Do you want another Cardigan or perhaps a different breed so as to avoid comparison with your beloved friend? Most people usually buy the same breed because they know (and love) the characteristics of that breed. Then, too, they often know people who have the same breed and perhaps they are lucky enough that one of their friends expects a litter soon. What could be better?

EUTHANASIA

Euthanasia must be performed by a licensed veterinary surgeon. There also may be societies for the prevention of cruelty to animals in your area. They often offer this service upon a vet's recommendation.

When you purchased your Cardigan Welsh Corgi, you should have made it clear to the breeder whether you wanted one just as a loveable companion and pet, or if you hoped to be buying a Cardigan with show prospects. No reputable breeder will sell you a young puppy saying that it is *definitely* of show quality, for so much can go wrong during the early months of a puppy's development. If you plan to show,

Training, proper care and responsible breeding pay off in the dog show ring. This well-put-together blue-merle Cardigan is proving his worth with his excellent movement and attitude.

what you will hopefully have acquired is a puppy with 'show potential.'

To the novice, exhibiting a Cardigan in the show ring may look easy but it takes a lot of hard work and devotion to do top winning at a show such as the prestigious Crufts Dog Show, not to mention a little luck too!

The first concept that the canine novice learns when watching a dog show is that each dog first competes against members of its own breed. Once the judge has selected the best member of each breed, provided that the show is judged on a Group system, that chosen dog will compete with other dogs in its group. Finally the best of each group will compete for Best in Show and Reserve Best in Show.

The second concept that you must understand is that the dogs are not actually competing against one another. The judge compares each dog against the breed standard, which is the written description of the ideal specimen of the breed. While some early breed standards were indeed based on specific dogs that were famous or popular, many dedicated enthusiasts say that a perfect specimen, described in the standard, has never walked into a show ring, has never been bred and, to the woe of dog breeders around the globe, does not exist. Breeders attempt to get as close to this ideal as possible, with every litter, but theoretically the 'perfect' dog is so elusive that it is impossible. (And if the 'perfect' dog were born, breeders and judges would never agree that it was indeed 'perfect.')

If you are interested in exploring dog shows, your best bet is to join your local breed club. These clubs often host both Championship and Open Shows, and sometimes Match meetings and special events, all of which could be of interest, even if you are only an onlooker. Clubs also send out newsletters and some organise training days and seminars in order that people may learn more about their chosen breed. To locate the breed club closest to you, contact The Kennel Club, the ruling body for the British dog world. The Kennel Club governs not only conformation shows but also working trials, obedience shows, agility trials and field trials. The Kennel Club furnishes the rules and regulations for all these events plus general dog registration and other basic requirements of dog ownership. Its annual show, the Crufts Dog Show, held in

WINNING THE TICKET
Earning a championship at Kennel Club shows is the most difficult in the world. Compared to the United States and Canada, where it is relatively not 'challenging,' collecting three green tickets not only requires much time and effort, it can be very expensive! Challenge Certificates, as the tickets are properly known, are the building blocks of champions—good breeding, good handling, good training and good luck!

Birmingham, is the largest benched show in England. Every year over 20,000 of the UK's best dogs qualify to participate in this marvellous show, which lasts four exciting days.

The Kennel Club governs many different kinds of shows in Great Britain, Australia, South Africa and beyond. At the most competitive and prestigious of these shows, the Championship Shows, a dog can earn Challenge Certificates (CCs), and thereby become a Show Champion or a Champion. A dog must earn three Challenge Certificates under three different judges to earn the prefix of 'Sh Ch' or 'Ch.' Note that some breeds must also qualify in a field trial in order to gain the title of full champion. Challenge Certificates are awarded to a very small percentage of the dogs competing, and dogs that are already Champions compete with others for these coveted CCs. The number of Challenge Certificates awarded in any one year is based upon the total number of dogs in each breed entered for competition.

There are three types of Championship Shows: an all-breed General Championship Show for all Kennel-Club-recognised breeds; a Group Championship Show that is limited to breeds within one of the groups; and a Breed Show that is usually confined to a single breed.

The Kennel Club determines which breeds at which Championship Shows will have the opportunity to earn Challenge Certificates (or tickets). Serious exhibitors often will opt not to participate if the tickets are withheld at a particular show. This policy makes earning championships even more difficult to accomplish.

Open Shows are generally less competitive and are frequently used as 'practice shows' for young dogs. There are hundreds of Open Shows each year that can be delightful social events and are great first show experiences for the novice. Even if you're considering just watching a show to wet your paws, an Open Show is a great choice.

While Championship and Open Shows are most important for the beginner to understand, there are other types of shows in which the interested dog owner can participate. Training clubs sponsor Matches that can be entered on the day of the show for a nominal fee. In these introductory-level exhibitions, two dogs are pulled out of a hat and 'matched,' the winner of that match goes on to the next round, and eventually only one dog is left undefeated.

Exemption Shows are much more light-hearted affairs with usually only four pedigree classes and several 'fun' classes, all of which can be entered on that day. Exemption Shows are sometimes held in conjunction with small agricultural shows and the proceeds must be given to a charity. Limited Shows are also available in small number, but entry is restricted to members of the club which hosts the show, although one can usually join the club when making an entry.

Before you actually step into the ring, you would be well advised to sit back and observe the judge's ring procedure. If it is your first time in the ring, do not be over-anxious and run to the front of the line. It is much better to stand back and study how the exhibitor in front of you is performing. The judge asks each handler to 'stand' the dog, hopefully showing the dog off to his best advantage. The judge will observe the dog from a distance and from different angles, approach the dog, check his teeth, overall structure, alertness and muscle tone, as well as consider how well the dog 'conforms' to the standard. Most importantly, the judge will have the exhibitor move the dog around the ring in some pattern that he or she should specify (another advantage to not going first, but always listen since some judges change their directions, and the judge is always right!). Finally the judge will give the dog one last look before moving on to the next exhibitor.

HOW TO ENTER A DOG SHOW

1. Obtain an entry form and show schedule from the Show Secretary.
2. Select the classes that you want to enter and complete the entry form.
3. Transfer your dog into your name at The Kennel Club. (Be sure that this matter is handled before entering.)
4. Find out how far in advance show entries must be made. Oftentimes it's more than a couple of months.

If you are not in the top three at your first show, do not be discouraged. Be patient and consistent and you may eventually find yourself in the winning line-up. Remember that the winners were once in your shoes and have devoted many hours and much money to earn the placement. If you find that your dog is losing every time and never getting a nod, it may be time to consider a different dog sport or just enjoy your Cardigan as a pet.

WORKING TRIALS

Working trials can be entered by any well-trained dog of any breed, not just Gundogs or Working dogs. Many dogs that earn the Kennel Club Good Citizen Dog award choose to participate in a working trial. There are five stakes at both open and championship levels: Companion Dog (CD), Utility Dog (UD), Working Dog (WD), Tracking Dog (TD) and Patrol Dog (PD). As in conformation shows, dogs compete against a standard and if the dog reaches the qualifying mark, it obtains a certificate. Divided into groups, each exercise must be achieved 70 percent in order for the dog to qualify. If the dog achieves 80 percent in the open level, it receives a Certificate of Merit (COM); in the championship level, it receives a Qualifying Certificate. At the CD stake, dogs must participate in four groups: Control, Stay, Agility

and Search (Retrieve and Nosework). At the next three levels, UD, WD and TD, there are only three groups: Control, Agility and Nosework.

Agility consists of three jumps: a vertical scale up a wall of planks; a clear jump over a basic hurdle with a removable top bar; and a long jump across angled planks.

To earn the UD, WD and TD, dogs must track approximately one-half mile for articles laid from one-half hour to three hours previously. Tracks consist of turns and legs, and fresh ground is used for each participant.

The fifth stake, PD, involves teaching manwork, which is not recommended for every breed.

HERDING TRIALS

Herding trials are popular among Cardigans and their owners. Breeders take great care in preserving the Cardigan's herding instinct and ability. The Cardigan is multi-talented in the field and his skills extend themselves to all types of livestock—fowl, sheep, cattle, etc. Many Cardigan breed clubs and owners arrange herding trials that are held all year 'round.

Buster, owned by Richard and Kathleen Hall, practising for an agility trial.

CLASSES AT DOG SHOWS

There can be as many as 18 classes per sex for your breed. Check the show schedule carefully to make sure that you have entered your dog in the appropriate class. The classes offered can include Minor Puppy (ages 6 to 9 months), Puppy (ages 6 to 12 months), Junior (ages 6 to 18 months) and Beginners (handler or dog never won first place), as well as the following, each of which is defined in the schedule: Maiden; Novice; Tyro; Debutant; Undergraduate; Graduate; Post-graduate; Minor Limit; Mid Limit; Limit; Open; Veteran; Stud Dog; Brood Bitch; Progeny; Brace and Team.

AGILITY TRIALS

Agility trials began in the United Kingdom in 1977 and have since spread around the world, especially to the United States, where they are very popular. The handler directs his dog over an obstacle course that includes jumps (such as those used in the working trials), as well as tyres, the dog walk, weave poles, pipe tunnels, collapsed tunnels, etc. Mini-agility has been devised as well so that small breeds can participate in this ever-growing sport. The obstacles are basically the same, but they are adjusted in size for smaller dogs. The Kennel Club requires that dogs not be trained for agility until they are 12 months old. This dog sport is great fun for dog and owner alike, and interested owners should join a training club that has obstacles and experienced agility handlers who can introduce you and your dog to the 'ropes' (and tyres, tunnels, etc.).

SHOW QUALITY SHOWS

While you may purchase a puppy in the hope of having a successful career in the show ring, it is impossible to tell, at eight to ten weeks of age, whether your dog will be a contender. Some promising pups end up with minor to serious faults that prevent them from taking home a Best of Breed award, but this certainly does not mean they can't be the best of companions for you and your family. To find out if your potential show dog is show quality, enter him in a match to see how a judge evaluates him. You may also take him back to your breeder as he matures to see what he might advise.

FÉDÉRATION CYNOLOGIQUE INTERNATIONALE

Established in 1911, the Fédération Cynologique Internationale (FCI) represents the 'world kennel club.' This international body brings uniformity to the breeding, judging and showing of pure-bred dogs. Although the FCI originally included only five European nations: France, Germany, Austria, the Netherlands and Belgium (which remains its headquarters), the organisation today embraces nations on six continents and recognises well over 300 breeds of pure-bred dog. There are three titles attainable through the FCI: the International Champion, which is the most prestigious; the International Beauty Champion, which is based on aptitude certificates in different countries; and the International Trial Champion, which is based on achievement in obedience trials in different countries. Dogs from every country can participate in these impressive canine spectacles, the largest of which is the World Dog Show, hosted in a different country each year. FCI sponsors both national and international shows. The hosting country determines the judging system and breed standards are always based on the breed's country of origin.

The FCI is divided into ten 'Groups.' At the World Dog Show, the following 'Classes' are offered for each breed: Puppy Class (6–9 months), Youth Class (9–18 months), Open Class (15 months or older) and Champion Class. A dog can be awarded a classification of Excellent, Very Good, Good, Sufficient and Not Sufficient. Puppies can be awarded classifications of Very Promising, Promising or Not Promising. Four placements are made in each class. After all sexes and classes are judged, a Best of Breed is selected. Other special groups and classes may also be shown. Each exhibitor showing a dog receives a written evaluation from the judge.

Besides the World Dog

DID YOU KNOW?

The FCI *does not* issue pedigrees. The FCI members and contract partners are responsible for issuing pedigrees and training judges in their own countries. The FCI does maintain a list of judges and makes sure that they are recognised throughout the FCI member countries.

The FCI also *does not* act as a breeder referral; breeder information is available from FCI-recognised national canine societies in each of the FCI's member countries.

FCI INFORMATION

There are 330 breeds recognised by the FCI, and each breed is considered to be 'owned' by a specific country. Each breed standard is a cooperative effort between the breed's country and the FCI's Standards and Scientific Commissions. Judges use these official breed standards at shows held in FCI member countries. One of the functions of the FCI is to update and translate the breed standards into French, English, Spanish and German.

Show, you can exhibit your dog at speciality shows held by different breed clubs. Speciality shows may have their own regulations.

My Cardigan Welsh Corgi

PUT YOUR PUPPY'S FIRST PICTURE HERE

Dog's Name _____

Date _____ Photographer _____